# SANAE FLOYD

SANAE FLOYD

# Table of Contents

SANAE FLOYD

# Acknowledgements

I dedicate this book to my children, Rebecca and Jake.

I would like to express gratitude to those people who have helped me on this incredible journey, whether they realised it or not!

Firstly Jeremy Meadowcroft, who has been, and continues to be my rock. His unwavering love and support, and his silent hugs during my melt-downs, have helped me so much. I love you Jem x

My angel coach, Hasnaa Akabli – who lovingly kept me on track as well as lovingly slapping my legs anytime I attempted to get off topic and avert the hard work involved!

Thank you! Thank you! Thank you!

My friends old and new:

Diane Hill, Sofia Pacifico-Reis, Joy Fisher, Abi Briant-Smith and Lucy Crane who encouraged and inspired me, who cried with me and cheered with me! I love you so much.

I want to express love and gratitude to my darling mum and her Paul – your faith in me is humbling.

To Abigail and her team at Authors & Co. I had no idea how I was going to make this all happen and in you swooped!! I'm grateful beyond words!

# Introduction

The late great Jim Rohn used to talk about the day that will change your life. A day that starts off like any other until something happens that alters the set of your sail.

Rohn tells the story of the day he lied to a Girl Scout who was selling girl scout cookies. He didn't have the $2 to buy a box from her so he told her that he'd already bought a box and still had plenty left.

After the Girl Scout thanked him and went on her way, Rohn was overcome with remorse and regret for the direction his life was heading. He was scraping by financially, he had mounting debts, a family to support and not a lot to feel proud of himself about. The day he lied to the girl scout was the day he decided to turn his life around.

I've had a number of those "enough is enough" days in my lifetime, as I'm sure you have too. Situations that jerked me out of a kind of waking slumber. Always challenging at the time, and yet looking back, always monumentally beautiful.

The evidence of those life-changing moments are all wrapped up in my current wonderful life with its abundance of love, friendships, my own business, fulfilling work, my health and my close and loving family.

The one area that has lurked in the background, that I spent years imagining I had a handle on when I didn't, was my debt situation. I have been in credit card debt, with an ever-growing balance, for 23 years and with a vice like stranglehold, that debt was slowly bringing me to my knees.

I didn't appreciate at the time quite how debilitating it was, until I started to shine a spot-light on that corner of my life and I saw how I was allowing it to completely diminish my capacity to experience joy.

When I started this project – to become Paid in Full and chronicle the journey - I was so full of shame and self-doubt. My self-worth was on the floor!

I didn't realise quite how exhausted I was and how burdened I was by my debt until I started to scratch beneath the surface and see what was really going on. I was emotionally spent and spinning my wheels believing I was doomed to a life of debt and dependency. Feeling foolish with a bookshelf laden with books about wealth and money, yet financially I was in a mess.

I had tried so many debt reduction strategies and repayment processes over the years. I'd get so far and then somehow wind up even deeper in debt than I was before. It was bewildering! Just like those stories of dieters who lose so much weight and feel wonderful, only to pile it all back on again within a matter of months!

I was confused, and my only conclusion was that I had no self-control. I guess too that I was waiting for some magic bullet that would someday blast my debt clear away.

I didn't realise that I was truly stuck in a holding pattern of negative thoughts and beliefs – a persistent and insidious pattern that was building up and creating a burden that was weighing heavier and heavier with each passing year.

At my turning point I didn't even know the amount of debt I had accumulated because I was too scared to face it. I was in state of denial – I knew it was bad but up to then I just felt too weak to face the reality of the mess I'd created.

I honestly thought that if I knew the full extent, I would find it too overwhelming and so I stuck my head in the sand and just hoped that my magic bullet (whatever that meant!) was going to show up soon!

I was deeply ashamed and every negative meaning that could ever be applied to credit cards and debt was dominant in my beliefs. What felt even more devastating was how my debt situation was impacting my coaching business.

It wasn't until I started this journey that I appreciated just how much my debt was affecting my ability to grow my business. As much as I believed I was 'showing up' and being authentic, truth was, there was huge part of me that remained in hiding! I had actually been playing so small!!

I felt ashamed, and out of integrity, because as a sales coach I was helping my clients make money and yet here I was deep in debt. I believed that I didn't have my shit together and so I constantly felt like a fraud. Despite the amazing results my clients were getting, I held back and hid so much of myself because I allowed my financial situation to define me.

As a result, I was driving my beloved business into a ditch and sabotaging my best efforts, and I felt helpless to stop it.

# The Turning Point

I maxed out my biggest credit card. In fact, a payment got declined because it took me over the £18k limit. I had other cards and they were already at their limits. I was devastated, and I felt I'd hit rock bottom.

Emotionally I began to unravel. I felt the blood drain from my face and I started crying uncontrollably. I didn't know what I was going to do.

I hadn't told a soul about my debt – I never talked about it because I was so embarrassed by it. How could I tell someone else when I was unable to face the truth for myself?

Then a few days after I'd maxed out my last card, I was having a catch- up conversation with another coach, we'd exchanged coaching services in the past and so there was a lovely bond between us. We were chatting about life and business and it was great, but I was struggling to focus. Inside I was like a pressure cooker and I knew I had to say something, to confide in someone, just to feel some relief! She sensed my agitation and asked me what was wrong…

I began talking! I told her about my debt situation and exactly how I was feeling about it. She listened intently, and do you know, I cannot remember what she said exactly but I can remember what I heard! I heard her say "people commit suicide over less, so you must be very strong"

# "People commit suicide over less {debt}, so you must be very strong"

That was my turning point. To this day, I have a gut feeling that she didn't *actually* say those words, which may seem strange to you, but I *had* to hear it in that way.  My brain interpreted it in the way that achieved maximum impact and drove my decision to do everything in my power to change my situation - once and for all.

So, as I surveyed my landscape, finding myself on my knees with a struggling business, deeper in debt than I'd ever been and filled with shame at how my life was turning out, I felt like a complete fraud and a failure.

At that moment an unfamiliar rage rose up inside of me. How could I have allowed myself to get to this point? Suddenly, I was livid! Spewing in fact! Where did I go wrong? I'm a smart woman! A high-achiever! I've got it all going on! Beautiful children, a loving and supportive family, my own home, an amazing boyfriend, and the freedom of my own business doing what I love!

Where was my power??!

As the fog of my anger cleared, I realised that nothing was going to change unless I changed. I had to take my power back. I had to take full responsibility for myself and my situation. I had to face up to some home-truths and dive deep into the root causes. I made a commitment to myself that day that enough was enough.

And that day was the day I decided that I was going to learn how to become debt-free forever.

I appreciate how very fortunate I am. I have a loving family and support, I have the wherewithal to understand that there is always a solution to every problem and I am healthy and able to work. Many people don't have all or any of these things, and so the burden of overwhelming debt can feel like one that is too great to bear.

So, I decided to chronicle the journey, to track my highs and lows and record my progress with a desire to help others. Not only were the coach's words ringing in my ears "people commit suicide over less…" but I knew of so many entrepreneurs who were crippled by their debts and as a result were unable to fully 'show up' in their businesses.

I thought if I could break my own 23-year love hate relationship with debt and change my circumstances, then surely this would serve others. I was excited by this prospect.

The Hawthorne Effect probably contributed to my success in staying the course, which did not carry a high probability based on my track record for starting things but then failing to see them through (more on this later!).

The Hawthorne Effect is where subjects who take part in an experiment, alter their behaviour because they're being observed. I felt like I was under the microscope for this endeavour, like I was the subject of an experiment. I logged, scrutinised and analysed my thoughts, feelings, behaviour and results every day.

What I didn't know, when I started this process was how much of an emotional and spiritual journey I was embarking on. I used to believe I needed smarter strategies and budgeting, but that's not the case.

I had to look within – deeper than I'd ever done before.

And the more I explored and understood, the more beautiful, liberating and awakening the experience. And this is available to everyone.

The first step to becoming debt free is to become emotionally free from the anxiety and stress. To gain mastery over your thoughts and emotions when it comes to money and debt. I worked on overcoming the toxic nature of my relationship with money and the old patterns and beliefs that were perpetuating the debt.

I had to overcome my slack mindset and my reliance on credit as a fall back.

When you are emotionally free, and the old negative patterns have been broken, then you can implement the strategies.

It's said that success in any area is 80% psychology and 20% strategy so to win at the 'game of life' you must master your mind.

This book is largely about that 80%. This is the biggest piece of work that any of us must do to affect any sort of transformation to achieve the results we want in life, and the emotionally charged subject of money and debt is no different.

It's been immense, exciting and exhilarating and my understanding of how powerful we all are is something that I've become totally passionate about sharing with everyone who wants to transform their lives and become Paid in Full once and for all!

Being Paid in Full starts in the mind and in the heart and is a state of being-ness that will bring so much lightness and joy.

I chose Paid In Full as my desired state, over 'debt free' because words are powerful and at the start of this journey, the word 'debt' was too heavily loaded with negativity for me.

I am a personal development junkie and I considered myself fluent in the Law of Attraction. Yet I felt a victim to my subconscious blocks because as much as I worked on my mindset and staying positive, my results were devastating in terms of my finances.

Throughout this process I discovered how to overcome my subconscious blocks and free myself from them forever!

True to form (I don't hang about) once I'd decided that I was going to do this, I took decisive action.

I got clear on exactly what I was dealing with in terms of the amount of debt I had, and I created a new spreadsheet detailing all of my incomings and outgoings, so I was clear on what I needed to make each month as a minimum.

As I write this now, it sounds like a mechanical activity that I just completed, without any emotion. Nothing could be further from the truth! In fact, my emotional response to *finally* facing up to the reality of the numbers was intensely painful. My whole body was shaking, and I was caught off guard by the intensity of my feelings!

I knew that I had to acknowledge my feelings and interpret the thoughts behind my intense emotions in order to eventually release them.

From the start I laid out my foundations of daily disciplines that I knew would be powerful for shifting my state from one of lack and fear, to empowered and prosperous. This part was fun and, as with any new endeavour, I felt fresh, excited and full of enthusiasm and hope.

I continued through a process of connecting my mind and body to really understand and interpret my thoughts and feelings around debt. I connected to shame in a really big way as the overriding emotion and the one that was keeping me stuck in a negative holding pattern.

I become a conscious observer of myself! I found *me* fascinating!

I played with my understanding of the powerful Law of Attraction and was enjoying some pretty fast results. Within a few short weeks I had signed new clients into my business and managed to repay 2 of my smaller credit cards and I was feeling great!

As with all processes of change, after that initial burst of excitement and positive results, I stumbled across some major internal road-blocks!

There were moments when I felt consumed with self-doubt and overwhelmed by negative mind-chatter. At the same time as I was taking the daily steps to break my debt habit and chronicle the journey, I was also working on breathing new life into my coaching business, so my work was cut out for me to learn to manage my emotions around all of this change.

I learned to become very adept at recognising resistance and interpreting the sabotaging behaviour that can show up when we're making progress towards our goals and as a result, I discovered ways to effectively overcome them.

Now, I'm not religious by any stretch of the imagination, I was raised by atheist parents and religious sermons would leave me bewildered and questioning *"does anyone really believe this stuff??"* Yet I'd always longed for some deeper sense of connection with a broader perspective and I believe, through this process, that I found what I was looking for.

Life started taking on a whole new meaning as I was beginning to appreciate the truth of my power to create my own reality.

Where I had previously felt helpless and victim to my subconscious patterns, I began to feel in control. I realised that my subconscious blocks are only an issue when they're 'active' and my results revealed whether they were active or not.

Wherever and whenever I experienced unwanted or unsatisfactory results I tuned into my feelings on the subject and interpreted the thoughts behind them. This level of conscious awareness gave me more control to overcome my self-limiting beliefs and create new results.

The more I learned about who I am, the more forgiving and compassionate I felt towards myself and the *mistakes* I'd made, and I moved into a state of increasing self-acceptance.

My debt balance diminished as I neutralised all my negativity around it, the stranglehold it had on my heart released. I no longer gave it any attention or energy, and this wasn't about denial or avoidance as it once had been, I just felt liberated to direct all my energy towards creating my best life NOW!

I'm thrilled to share my journey with you and impart my learnings, that have changed my life for the better in every way! In sharing the most vulnerable parts of my story, and printing some of the highlights from my own journal, my wish is that this inspires you to embark on your own empowering path.

All you need is yourself and your own journal. Enjoy! You are more powerful than you realise.

With love

Sanae x

# The Power of Decision

For whatever reason, I had to wake up in a ditch in order to garner the motivation to commit to changing my financial situation. I guess it was because I was in a state of denial, too ashamed to face up to my reality and possibly still hoping, wishing, praying that my luck would somehow change.

I knew I didn't want anyone else to bail me out – it wasn't as though I was seeking a knight in shining armour. I wanted to experience the pride and satisfaction of repaying all of my debt myself, by my own means and yet I wasn't doing anything about it!

Well, actually, that's not entirely true. Much of my debt had been accumulated by investment into my business - in programme's and business coaching. It wasn't a lack of strategy that I was suffering from when it came to making enough money to not only live, but also pay off my debts.

I had experienced success in my on-line coaching business but for whatever reason I was bumping up against an invisible ceiling on my income. Then in the 12 months leading up to starting this journey, I had been spiralling down-hill, and at the time I didn't know why. I felt completely out of control and I was looking externally for answers. I was terrified if I'm honest.

I threw more money into my business. I was seeking some magic bullet outside of myself that would give me everything I wanted and set me on my path to financial freedom!

I realise now that there is no magic bullet outside of myself. That in order to change my situation, I had to look within and change myself.

The first thing I had to do was to DECIDE. I made a decision to become Paid In Full.

The impact of a decision is so powerful!

I'd spent literally decades of my life trying to get a handle on my finances and pay off my debt and yet I always failed, and I didn't have the first clue why.

I know now that I hadn't really committed to the decision to become debt free. I always had one foot in the "I really want to be debt free" camp and the other foot in the "Yes, but, it's too hard" camp and the internal conflict was keeping me stuck.

You see there's a huge gulf between *wanting* to achieve something and *deciding* to achieve something.

In that gulf exists fear, limitation and excuses. Reasons to stay in bed, instead of getting up and taking massive positive action! But, by actually deciding, you're leaping over that gulf and committing. It's empowering, and it changes everything.

A decision takes you out of the realms of limiting beliefs and internal conflict because you're making an assertion, setting an intention, that cuts you off from all alternatives – you're burning the bridges to take the island, so to speak.

The derivation of the word "decide" is literally "to sever" or "cut off".

Once you empower yourself with a decision, you embolden your state of mind and begin to think differently. A decision refines your focus on what it is that you want to achieve. You've leapt and if you don't start moving forward towards the goal, you'll fall. It requires massive action and doing things differently.

I remember listening to an interview with Bob Proctor and he said something that I'd never really considered until this significant moment.

Bob was talking about a couple who were telling him how much they'd love to buy a property on the coast.

Bob asked them *"Why don't you buy it then, if you love it so much?"*

They retorted *"We don't have the money! We can't afford those prices!"* and Bob replied, *"You don't need the money!"*

The couple were confused (as was I at that point!) and asked *"What do you mean? Of course we need the money!"* and Bob said *"You don't need the money to buy the house, because you haven't yet decided to buy the house!"*

The couple were stuck in the gulf between wanting and deciding, where, as I said earlier, limitations and excuses exist. They didn't need the money because they hadn't *decided* to buy the house. If they made the decision to buy the house, they would free themselves from the gulf, so they could move forward and take the required action to raise the money.

Bob concluded this interview by sharing that this couple made a decision and within 12 months they were in their dream home on the coast.

I have made many key decisions in my life – times when I've leapt and, as they say, grew my wings on the way down.

My business is one such example. I resigned from my respectable 9-5 job in the financial services industry (I know! The Irony…) to start my coaching business with no clue how I was going to make it happen. But I had decided that I was going to create a business of my own and that was all I needed to start.

The 'how' shows up. Your brain is like a goal seeking missile and as soon as you've committed to your 'what' and you've leapt that gulf, your brain starts working for you – seeking out the 'how' - and you start getting the ideas, possibilities and resources to help you get moving.

Rarely, in this monumental moment of decision is there fear or doubt. There's just excitement, relief and a renewed energy and enthusiasm for life.

And no better place to start.

# Backing the 'What' with a 'Why'

Once you've made the decision, it's time to strengthen your resolve with clarity of purpose. I'm talking about backing your decision with a powerful 'why'.

When I gave my desire to be Paid in Full a deeper sense of meaning, my commitment was fueled with the energy of excitement and I had something to focus on that was fun, important to me and underpinned so many of my values (I'll talk about values a little later).

Research shows that intrinsic motivation is way more powerful than any external motivation, such as a promise of reward. When we are driven by intrinsic motivations, we are more effective, more creative and more successful.

Your personal and powerful "why" will keep your skin in the game when the going gets tough – when you feel like giving up or in a weaker moment you question yourself and wonder "is this really worth it?", it's your 'why' that holds you steady and grounded.

# "He who has a why to live can bear almost any how"

**Friedrich Nietzsche**

In ALL areas of my life I have always achieved exactly what I wanted – no matter how hard the work, the toil and the tears, I always achieve my goals and yet my debt goal has always alluded me.

I realise now that with all my other accomplishments, from passing exams to running the London Marathon and to starting my own business, not only was I *decided* but I also had a clear sense of purpose.

I could clearly see the 'why' behind the 'what' of each one of my goals. Which meant that even when I was tempted to stay in bed instead of getting up at 5am to revise or to don my trainers to train I was compelled by the bigger picture, the real results.

I never had that with my debt repayment goals. Paying off my credit cards was the extent of the purpose but clearly as much as I was in emotional pain, just paying them off for the sake of paying them off was not a big enough driver. And clearly neither was the pain. The pain just kept me stuck and fearful.

To chronicle my journey, become published and help millions of people joyfully move themselves to freedom from debt - now THAT was a purpose that lit me up like a pin-ball machine! My big why was so much more than just paying off my debt and that gave me the lift I needed during those doubtful moments when I'd question my ability to achieve my goal.

**Call to Action:**

**<u>Define your big why</u>**

**What makes being Paid in Full a must for you?**

**How will it change your life for the better?**

**What will you feel more able to do as a result of becoming Paid in Full?**

**What will be the impact on your life, your health, wealth and well-being of becoming Paid in Full?**

**Who else will benefit from your changed circumstance and your freedom from the burden that you're currently carrying?**

**Get crystal clear on the why behind your decision and write it down. Keep it close to you and read it daily. This will tap into your positive emotional state and help you stay motivated to keep going, even when things feel tough.**

**Having a strong reason for doing something will compel you forward and keep you excited and enthused.**

*DAY 1 Journal excerpt:*

So, today is day 1 of my journey to freedom from debt. I have no idea what this will look like, but I have decided enough is enough. I am drawing a line in the sand.

I am taking my power back.

As I have made a conscious decision to choose to believe that I create my own reality I am choosing to believe that this has happened for me not to me. That this is all a part of the story that will enable me to help other men and women out of their personal debt crisis.

In making the decision and feeling excited to embark on this new journey a significant memory has been stirred.

I remember how 6 months ago I got excited at a thought that perhaps I will one day speak from a stage and share my story of how I got myself out of my personal debt situation. I felt elation as I imagined myself on a mission to help as many people as I could free themselves from their own crippling debt situations. Clearly a thought that has been percolating!

Within 24 hours of making the decision I visualised the front cover of this book – the red stamp with 'Paid In Full' emblazoned on the front. The visualisation was so exciting to me and I felt my whole-body tingling with excitement. This gives my journey real purpose!

And it starts now.

My declaration from today is that I have total control and I have EVERYTHING I need to make a debt free life my reality.

I am also focusing more on the feeling of accomplishment and pride as I announce to Jeremy and to my friends and to my coach that "I have done it!! I am PAID IN FULL!" I am focusing on the joy I'll be feeling as I can show up with integrity and share my story without shame.

I also need to figure out another 'Why?'.

Why am I in the situation at all? I need to get underneath the bonnet of my consciousness and uncover whatever attachment and association I have around money and debt that has created my reality and has perpetuated it for so many years despite my clear desire to not be in debt.

So, there we have it. In terms that Napoleon Hill would have been proud of I have my definite goal backed by purpose and burning desire. My purpose is to help other people get out of their perpetual debt cycle and become free like me!

# Facing the Truth

Periodically, over the years, I would pull out my credit card statements and make a list of the balances of each one in a vain attempt to get control.

But I always left off the smaller balances, those that were less than £2k. I also didn't acknowledge my £3.5k overdraft.  As illogical as that sounds, I just couldn't face the **whole** truth. Those smaller balances sure as hell added up! Yet I couldn't bring myself to acknowledge them, as though they breached my tipping point and therefore it was safer to ignore them.

As with any journey – not only do we need to be clear on the destination – it's essential to know the starting point.

Imagine setting off on a long journey to a new destination. Somewhere you've never been before. You key the destination in to your GPS and the first thing your GPS does is calibrate your starting point – it must know where you are in order to effectively guide your journey.

It's the same with your debt-free goal. If you're anything like I was, and you've not been completely open and honest with yourself about the extent of your debt, now is the time. I've got your back. The fact of the matter is that when you can face the truth, you're empowering yourself.

By lying and hiding the facts from yourself, you're sending a message to your brain that says, "I'm weak and I can't handle this" and that affects who you're being moment to moment. It erodes your confidence and self-belief which impacts your ability to take positive action.

It's time to take your power back, since you've made your decision and you have renewed purpose and meaning behind your decision, now is the time to get crystal clear on what you're dealing with.

**Call to Action:**

**Empower yourself with clarity. Affirm continuously if you need to "I'm taking my power back" as you list all of your outstanding balances owing, in full, omitting none.**

Appreciate yourself for taking bold honest action and acknowledge the fact that the total figure you've arrived at is going to reduce and reduce and reduce.

Create an excel spreadsheet with all of your outgoings and incomings so you have a clear picture of exactly how much you need as a minimum every single month.

# Acknowledging 'What Is'

Having immersed myself in personal growth and development in earnest for over 4 years, I understood the concept that nothing has meaning but the meaning we attach to it. The problem was my negative association to debt was so deeply ingrained and loaded with intense emotion that I couldn't seem to get any healthy perspective on it.

In a bid to shift my perspective, my previous coaches and friends would say to me *"the credit companies trust you and see you as a good money manager and that's why they granted you the credit card"* and *"wealthy people have credit cards too"*.

I'd hear myself replying ***"I know, you're right, thank you"*** to stop them talking because inside I was screaming ***"But I hate myself for having this debt!"***

No amount of reasoning conversation was going to shift my vantage point. I needed to confront my truth head on and that meant not denying my feelings but instead interpreting and understanding them.

**How we think determines how we feel. How we feel determines our actions and behaviours and our actions and behaviours drives our results**

Acknowledging 'what is' means fully embracing where you are right now and becoming sensitive to your feelings. Feelings exist to be felt but often we're rushing around either too busy or too afraid to really feel our emotions.

We try to numb our bad feelings by spending more money or with food or alcohol but as the formidable Brene Brown says "we can't selectively numb". In our attempts to numb the bad stuff, we also numb our ability to fully experience the good stuff!

In acknowledging 'what is' in the context of your current debt situation, allow yourself to feel the feelings that are coming up when you acknowledge your debt and, quite literally, *sit with them*. They're likely to feel painful and upsetting. But feel assured that as you acknowledge them and feel them, you're going to be able to, over time, rationalise your thought process and neutralise your emotions.

In the beginning of my journey, acknowledging 'what is' meant not avoiding the truth of my situation and therefore not avoiding the painful feelings.

Avoidance has been a major part of the problem for me. I chose not to face my debt because I didn't want to experience the negative emotion that surged whenever I did. Feelings such as shame and guilt overwhelmed me, and I feared the intensity of these emotions, so avoidance was my solution.

This was also the root of much of my misunderstanding of The Law of Attraction. I believed that by simply avoiding the problem, it would go away.

But you see, that's where I was going wrong for all these years. There's effort in avoidance and for me, it was actually a lot of hard mental and emotional effort to pretend there was no problem. There was fear coursing through my veins when I was in avoidance.

The joy was fake.

My need to avoid was fuelled by shame, and in feeling so acutely ashamed by the nature of The Law of Attraction (more on the law coming up next) I was continually attracting more into my experience to feel ashamed about, and that included more debt.

As I faced up to the reality of my situation I focused inwardly on my body and allowed myself to experience the feelings.

I set aside some time when I knew I would not be disturbed, and I focused in on my feelings when I looked at my debt. It was distinctly uncomfortable, but as I stayed with it, I started to gain clarity. As I sat with my eyes closed, I placed my attention where there was the most intense feeling.

It felt like a blockage in my solar plexus and my heart was aching. I sat and acknowledged my body and these feelings and after a short while I felt somehow separated from my body, like I was just observing it. I suppose that's all I was doing, just observing, noticing and acknowledging.

It never occurred to me until I started this journey that the bad feeling I experienced when I looked at my mounting debt, wasn't really about the debt itself, but rather all the meaning that I'd placed on it. I had so many negative stories and beliefs about what that debt represented and what it reflected about me and my personality.

Once I was able to observe the feelings, I was able then to isolate them and label them which meant I could unravel the stories and beliefs that were behind these intense feelings. This gave me the best vantage point to then begin the process of replacing them with more empowering beliefs.

*DAY 1 Continued:*

I feel like crying right now. My heart is aching, and I am feeling overwhelmed with shame as I acknowledge the truth.

Deep breathe. Here goes!

Right now, I am £47788 in debt across various credit cards, an overdraft and money I owe to my mum. What a mess!

I have been in debt from the moment I was able to apply for credit. When I was 18, I left home to go to Bradford University. Such an exciting and liberating time. It was a time when there was a clear division between townies and students – townies had money. Students embraced the poverty mindset!! We were proud! I'm sure most of us deliberately dressed down in full respect of our student status!

As the banks enticed us with their branded flyers and banners, I walked straight into Natwest and applied for my student loan. The full £800 that I was entitled too. I can't even remember why. In those days we received grants and my parents funded me – my mum paid me a monthly standing order and it wrenches my gut to think about that now. She was supporting me, and I was still wanting MORE.

So that's the start. 18 years old. Not a care in the world. Credit available to me without any knowledge of how I was ever going to repay it. I wasn't thinking about how I'd repay it, I just believed that I would very easily pay it all back once I was working.

What did I spend it on?

In that first year I paid for driving lessons and got my driver's licence. Sensible I guess. Oh! And I went to Egypt for 3 weeks with my best friend, Diane. Looking back, how the hell did I explain that one to my parents???

Fresh from the summer holiday to Egypt, I returned to Bradford for the start of year 2 and I walked straight into the bank again and applied for my next "hit". This time it was a little more, £950. What did I do with that money? I spent 3 weeks in the summer of 1995 in New York and Chicago with another friend.

And of course, in year 3 I applied again. By the end of my 3 years at university, I had £3000 in student loan debt and I'd already applied for my first credit card. I realise that by today's standards, that amount is miniscule, but the point is, it was unnecessary.

So, there you have it, the start of a 23-year relationship with 'bad debt'. With no apparent justification.

My appreciation for this easy money turned sour very quickly. As soon as I started earning money, I resented paying for stuff that I had already enjoyed (years ago) with money I was earning today. I began to get quite obsessed with paying off my debts. Every year amongst my New Years' Resolutions was "pay off credit cards." E-v-e-r-y year!

And every year the credit card balances were creeping UP instead of going down. Yet, I never addressed why that was happening.

Until today.

I'm 42 years old and I have £47788 in debt. £37788 owed on credit cards and an overdraft and £10k owed to my mum. As I write this, I'm experiencing a prickly sensation on the surface of my skin and my stomach is lurching.

There are only 2 people in the world right now who are aware of the extent of my situation. They are me and my new coach, Hasnaa. Not my partner, not my parents. Just me and Hasnaa.

In fact, just 24 hours ago, I was not even aware of this exact figure myself because I dared not acknowledge it. I knew it was getting bad. But I couldn't face it. Occasionally I would declare "I'm going to reclaim control" but still I didn't acknowledge where I was fully.

I spent time tuning in to my feelings like this almost every day in the first few weeks. I would just spend time focusing inwardly on my physical responses to money and my debt – giving space and acknowledging those feelings – and allowing whatever thoughts to emerge.

DAY 2:

As I experience so much conflict around my debt, I abhor it and yet I'm continually perpetuating more, I feel my body in a heightened hyper-vigilant state. I'm experiencing fear, discomfort and frustration.

How could I have let this happen?

Which leads me to see how there is a part of myself that I hate and reject. I hate and reject the part of me that gets myself into debt!

There is so much shame. Which is the reason I haven't been able to talk to anyone with specifics. Jeremy (my partner) knows I have debt and a couple of close friends, but they don't know the extent of it. How could they? I didn't even know!

The shame I feel is of someone who is out of control, who can't manage herself and her money, someone who can't say no, someone who is greedy and undisciplined.

All representing my negative associations with my debt situation – all creating such an emotional swirl that is clouding my judgment and causing me the anxiety and stress.

So, you see, I had subconsciously defined myself as a loser, as someone who is greedy, undisciplined and out of control when it comes to money. No wonder I felt bad! Once I knew that these were my beliefs, I could focus on changing them.

I started to enjoy being a conscious observer of my every emotion. I started to play with it. If I was engaged in an activity, or in a conversation and I experienced some strong negative emotion, I would mentally dial in to the feeling and ponder it. As I allowed the feeling to be felt, I asked myself *"What is the thought behind this feeling?"*

In 'being with' my feelings and allowing them to rise to the surface, I also recognised a pattern of chronic people pleasing, that had been previously beneath the surface of my conscious awareness. I wanted approval from others and I strived to be 'impressive' all the time which meant that I struggled to say 'no'.

When my friends invited me to events that meant spending more money than I had, I didn't think twice about using my credit cards so that I could say 'yes' and go.

When it came to birthdays and Christmas, I'd spend a fortune on presents and, again, without thinking I used my credit cards.

Even when I was being 'sold' to, I would never just say *"no thank you"* to the sales person, instead, I would come up with a silly, long-winded tale about how *"I just need to go somewhere right now but I'll definitely be back…"* even if I had no intention of going back!

Every time I got clarity on the negative thoughts and limiting beliefs that were driving the intense feelings I celebrated! Day by day I was becoming more self-aware and in control and more compassionate with myself. I realised how much my bogus beliefs had ruled my life and now I was taking my power back!

Over time the intensity of the emotions diminished until I was able to consider my debt without any negative emotion. Changing your stories and beliefs about debt, and accepting the truth that debt really has no meaning except the meaning you have given it means you can begin to take your power back.

Having a neutral perspective also means you can implement the strategies that ensures repayment and a healthier relationship with money in general

**Call to Action:**

**Set aside 15 – 30 minutes of undisturbed quiet time and have your journal to hand.**

**Either look at your credit card statements or just think about your current debt situation and notice when you start to feel those all too familiar negative emotions.**

**Close your eyes and mentally scan your body up and down a few times and then**

allow your attention to rest on the place where you're feeling the most intensity. It could be in the pit of your stomach or your chest; it may be a sensation in your throat or an ache in your heart.

Focus on the feeling and ask yourself:

*What are the thoughts fueling this feeling?*

*What I am saying to myself that is making me feel these feelings?*

*What is my belief right now?*

Sometimes it helps to intensify the feeling in order to jog the subconscious into revealing the buried beliefs. I do this by picturing a dial with the numbers 0-10 on it, rather like a combination dial on a safe, on my feelings. I then imagine turning the dial on my feelings up and as I do that, the feeling intensifies. I like to think of this process as really grabbing the attention of my subconscious, making it sit up and take notice!

Take as long as you need – you're truly giving yourself a magical gift of awareness. As thoughts and beliefs start emerging, write them in your journal.

This is important as it takes them out of your head and onto paper, so you can step back and view them with more objectivity.

Are these thoughts and beliefs serving you? NO!

So now you can begin to write the new thoughts and beliefs that you'd like to think instead, and place all of your focus on them until they become a part of you (more on this coming up!)

# The Law of Attraction

What I have appreciated and loved most about this journey is my deepening understanding of The Law of Attraction. I have come to a profound level of awareness of my own power when it comes to creating my reality and I am on a mission to share this with you, so you can experience the magic for yourself.

The Law of Attraction is a governing law of the universe that states we are living in a vibrational universe and that 'like attracts like'.

Every thought has a measurable frequency, a vibration, that goes out into the universe. That vibration attracts experiences, situations, circumstances and even other people that are a match to that frequency.

Positive thoughts attract positive experiences and negative thoughts attract negative experiences, therefore it's important to train your thoughts and focus positively on what you want.

You're never not thinking!

Research shows that we have in excess of 60,000 thoughts per day!! That's hard to monitor and manage moment to moment! And much of our thinking is at a subconscious level – we're not entirely aware of what we're thinking because we're just running along conditioned habits of thought. Our beliefs are just habitual ways of thinking that have become ingrained within us.

Fortunately, we have an internal guidance system – an inbuilt navigational system that tells us where we're heading without our having to try to control all our thoughts in every moment. This clever internal guidance system is how we **feel.**

When you feel bad – sad, angry, frustrated, overwhelmed, ashamed – you are off track and thinking negative thoughts. You're emitting a low vibration frequency that will attract more of the same - more to feel bad about.

When you feel good – joyful, satisfied, content, at peace, purposeful, passionate – you're going to attract more of the same.

Your job is to practice feeling good, more of the time!

Back in 2013 when I first started my personal development journey, after my life had completely unraveled following my marriage breakdown, I came across Rhonda Byrne's film "The Secret" which is all about The Law of Attraction.

I absolutely loved it, it spoke straight to my heart and I watched it repeatedly. I wanted to flood every cell in my body with this knowledge. Looking back, I just hoped so much to be a master at creating my own reality but there was a lot of doubt in the simplicity of it all. Now I realise that its power lies in its simplicity.

Whenever I thought about my debt, I was attracting more debt. Even when I was thinking in terms of "not wanting this debt" and wishing I was "debt free" I was still focused on debt.

When I looked at my credit card statements, my thoughts were so negative that I felt ashamed and out of control. That was my dominant vibration for so long, so it's no surprise that I continued to attract more to feel ashamed and out of control about.

When you feel good, anything that is not on the same positive 'feel good' vibrational frequency just falls under your radar and you don't notice it, or you notice it, but you don't dwell on it. It kind of bounces off of you.

I remember mum and I went to Japan when I was 18 years old. I lived in Bradford as a student and mum lived in London. We had a wonderful time – everyone was falling over themselves to make us comfortable and the hospitality was out of this world. We smiled and laughed all day every day and the sights, sounds and smells just felt strangely familiar.

It was Christmas time and the winter sun was bright and where there was snow, everything glimmered and glistened. It was so joyful.

Then we flew back into London and mum and I said our tearful goodbyes and I returned to Bradford. I felt so sad because I didn't want to leave Japan and mum and I are so close, and we laugh all the time and I instantly missed her company. Over the course of the next few days, I felt low.

I started criticising everything. My attention seemed to attach to things I hadn't noticed before – the faults and state of disrepair in the student digs seemed to leap out at me and annoy me, I got frustrated by the mess of my housemates (that previously didn't bother me) and the grey January drizzle felt heavier than ever before.

After a few days I dragged myself to the shops and met with the rudest shop assistant imaginable. Oh, she was sooo RUDE!! Then in the next shop I realised at the checkout that I'd dropped and lost the £10 note that was in my pocket. Unbelievable!! I wanted to cry.

I felt so embittered that I went to the nearest payphone (remember them?) and rang my mum and declared "*I hate it here!*!"

When the January term lectures re-started, and everyone returned from the holidays in high spirits my mood lifted, and I started to feel happy again. Suddenly, I stopped being bothered by the state of the student digs or the mess of my housemates – it all just disappeared into the background and was no longer a part of my reality.

I never saw that shop assistant again even though I was a frequent shopper in that particular store and I received a gift of money from my mum out of the blue with a note that read: "treat yourself to something nice to cheer you up".

I felt low for a few days and it really shaped my perspective of my reality and the experience I attracted in!

And so, here's the thing. That low mood was only temporary. But what if I'd stubbornly held it there for longer?

I had experiences that matched my "I don't want to be here" thoughts. My loyal and obedient brain noticed everything that backed up my thought like the states of disrepair and mess in the student house and the grey days and my low frequency attracted in experiences to match in the form of a rude shop assistant and the lost money.

If I held that thought for longer, it would become a belief. A belief is just a habit of thought, but our beliefs dictate our behaviours and our behaviours determine our results.

And as the belief takes hold it gains momentum. It gets stronger and becomes a dominant vibration because Law of Attraction will continually produce evidence that reinforces the belief and so we get stuck.

And that is what happened to me that perpetuated my debt. The dominant vibration of shame and guilt just brought me more of the same. And as I surveyed more of the same, I attracted more of the same…and on and on it went…until the blessed day of the decision.

Making significant changes in your life experience requires changing your habits of thought and re-writing those stories that you've got going on. In order to change your habits of thought and re-write your stories you must change your focus.

As simple as it sounds, it really starts here:

Instead of focusing on lack and scarcity, focus on and affirm abundance and prosperity.

Instead of focusing on sadness, focus on and affirm joy.

Instead of focusing on impatience, focus on and affirm appreciation.

Instead of focusing on powerlessness, focus on and affirm empowerment.

Instead of focusing on confusion, focus on and affirm clarity.

Instead of focusing on inertia, focus on and affirm productivity.

Instead of focusing on tired, focus on and affirm vitality.

Instead of focusing on hustle and grind, focus on and affirm more fun and play.

You have a choice moment to moment to direct your focus and start noticing the evidence of your new desires and your new story.

My first step to shifting my state on a more consistent basis was to practice gratitude every single day. Gratitude puts you in a state of appreciation for what you have now and as you focus on appreciating what you have now, the law of attraction brings you more of the same – that is yet more to feel appreciative of.

*"When you apply the idea of gratitude to Newton's law {of motion: Every action always has an opposite and equal reaction} it says: every action of <u>giving</u> thanks always causes an opposite reaction of* **receiving.** *And what you receive will always be equal to the amount of gratitude you've given. The means that the very action of gratitude sets off a reaction of receiving! And the more sincerely and the more deeply grateful you feel... the more you will receive"*

**Rhonda Byrne The Magic.**

Expressing gratitude also improves your mood and diminishes stress. As you're focusing on and appreciating everything that is good in your life, you create a positive internal shift in your hormone levels. The stress hormone, cortisol, reduces and you body releases feel-good hormones, serotonin, dopamine and endorphins, into your system.

When you're stressed out, oxygen flow is restricted to the pre-frontal cortex, which is the centre of logic and reasoning in your brain. You may feel "woolly" and unable to think clearly. Stress is a killer of creativity and resourcefulness because when you're stressed, you're operating in fight or flight mode. Which means you're naturally switched on to anything and everything that threatens your survival, and this is why you experience fear and anxiety.

You have to exercise deliberate and practised focusing, to overcome this default response, which is where a daily gratitude practice is critical. I promise you, as you do this every day, you will experience incredible shifts in your reality very quickly!

## DAY 2

It's going to take mental, emotional and physical fitness to achieve my goal. So much of the toughness does come from taking control of our physical fitness and I know personally that when I'm out running, I feel amazing.

Running helps me to feel such clarity and mental tenacity as well as physically strong. I also seem to generate a ton of ideas for content for my live-streams and my blog posts when I'm out there pounding the streets!

I haven't been running for such a long time! It's annoying how powerfully beneficial I find it and yet it's the first thing I drop when I feel stressed and overwhelmed.

Anyway, I shall incorporate exercise in to my daily schedule with immediate effect.

I remembered this morning how when I was journaling every single day and doing my gratitude practice {when I started my business 3 years earlier}, I would mark the days off and it would usually take 30 days before I started to manifest the results I wanted. It was amazing!

I remember how I'd feel great and so happy! You'd imagine that I'd keep up the practice that brought me those happy results as a matter of priority wouldn't you!! But I never kept it up. I'd get a few more weeks in and then I'd start to waiver and faulter and inadvertently lose interest, and momentum. I don't know why.

Perhaps, at the time I felt good and so I'd relax and become lazy? Or the daily words lost a bit of impact so it's not as powerful and therefore not as enjoyable?

The important point here is that I must re-introduce my daily mindset practice.

## Daily Gratitude Practice

Every day I list 10 things for which I'm blessed and grateful for. I give THANKS For what is coming.

Not only expressing gratitude for what is already received but practicing expressing thanks for what is desired, as though it's already received.

Thank you Thank you Thank you – the rule of 3 according to Rhonda Byrne is an important number in the creative process. Say Thank you Thank you Thank you – 3 times so you're really savouring the words and the feelings instead of just paying lip service.

Thank you Thank you Thank you for the income I received which has enabled me to complete my book "PAID IN FULL" and have it published.

DAY 3

When I look at my bank balance and it's a negative figure, I feel bad. Who wants to feel bad, right? Those bad feelings are indicative of my negative associations with debt. What does it say about me?

It says I'm "out of control", I'm "unable to manage myself". I'm "undisciplined and disorganised".

Wow!! No wonder I've avoided going there!

I need to re-wire my thinking to shift these thoughts!! If I'm running around with these beliefs, then I'll never be able to take the action to clear the debt. And the longer I stay in debt, the more I'll perpetuate these beliefs.

So as from today, I'm setting a daily reminder on my phone to check my bank balance. My bank balance is over-drawn, and I can't remember the last time it went into a credit position. However, when I look at the balance every day, I will consider 3 other areas in my life where I am abundant.

I will do this for at least the next 21 days – the time it takes to replace an old habit with a new habit.

The intention behind this is to build my positive associations when I look at my bank balance and also, I will be taking control and disproving my "I'm undisciplined" belief because I'll be doing it every day.

## DAY 6

For the past 2 days I have been practising thanking the Universe in advance for magical experiences in my day and expressing gratitude for the great news coming to me.

For example, I expressed gratitude for my journey to the dentist being a smooth one, I expressed thanks for the wonderful engagement in my Facebook community that I wanted to experience, and I expressed gratitude in advance for the new client signing up with me (as I did have a discovery call booked in)

I received all those things and so much more!! I had so much lively engagement in my Facebook community which is perfect!!

Thank you! Thank you! Thank you!

I signed a new client into my 4-month package. I radiated clarity and confidence in my offering and my ability to help and she said "yes!"

Clarity, confidence, focus and gratitude are so powerful!

Feeling good first is essential, so I'm going to get my nails done and go for a run. Focus! Focus! Focus! Focus on everything I want.

I booked an appointment with Abi, my homeopath today to clear the niggly pain I'm getting in my hip. As I did so I expressed happiness to pay for her services. I hesitated briefly as I thought about paying the fee, but then I remembered that I am valuing myself by taking care of my body and appreciating my desire to get to the root of the niggle in my hip before it gets any worse.

Magically, she asked me if I'd be happy to do a session trade as she would like my coaching services as she requires some clarity! She values my services highly, and this was demonstration that I am worth more that I give myself credit for. This is such a wonderful sign of abundance.

Jem {Jeremy} and I went out for a meal to celebrate my new client and I celebrated the abundance of lovely food and drink! Thank you, Jem, for sharing in my joy!

I am abundant! I also generously tipped the creative genius in FIVERR who created this book cover!!

## Call to Action:

### Daily gratitude practice:

**Every day list 10 things for which you are grateful and the reasons why you're grateful for it, to give the list real meaning to you.**

**Every morning give thanks in advance for the day going well with details of how it will go well for you i.e. the traffic being**

**free flowing and your client calls going well.**

**Set an alarm prompt, to look at your bank account balance every day and as you do so, focus on 3 areas of abundance such as the abundance of laughter in your friendships, the abundance of food in your fridge, of hot running water, of the autumn leaves on the trees that are so beautiful.**

We want what we want because we believe that we will feel happier when we have it. We're really chasing the feeling.

We want to be happy, we want to feel joy, love and prosperity. We want to feel abundant and successful and we believe that we will feel that when we have the *'stuff'* – the money, the house overlooking the sea, the thriving business.

In my capacity as a sales coach I teach my clients that people make all their buying decisions emotionally. We all do. We justify the purchase with logic but ultimately the driving force in our decision making is how it makes us feel, or how we believe we will feel once we have it.

ther you want to bask in prosperity or you
it to experience the feeling of security and
peace of mind, your job is to feel good and raise
your vibration to match the higher frequencies
of your desires.

To feel the good feelings of your desires
as though they are already manifested.

Your desire for more money so you can free
yourself from your debt and say yes to more
of want you want means raising your
vibration to become a match to more money.

How do you do this?

By training yourself to focus deliberately on
money, and not the lack of it. To notice and
acknowledge all the money that is flowing to
you. To surround yourself with images of
money and flood your subconscious with
affirmative statements of appreciation and
faith.

When you are deliberately looking for signs
of money and abundance coming to you,
guess what? You find it everywhere! From
coins in the street, to money in pockets of
jackets you haven't worn for months, to
vouchers for free coffee and discount
coupons on your favourite things! It all
represents the energetic vibration of money!

Acknowledge when your friend offers
to buy you lunch or when you receive a
gift of any sort.

See this as playing a game – you're
seeking out all the signs of
abundance that are everywhere
and all around you.

# *"There's gold dust in the air!"*

## Catherine Ponder

Pictures of money, post-it notes with
affirmations on your fridge, your mirror
and on your phone are all ways to flood
your subconscious and help you exercise
the muscle of focus.

What you focus on expands. The law of
attraction will see to that. Your thoughts are
powerful and as you think appreciative
thoughts of money,

you will attract more positive thoughts,
create more positive energy and receive the
ideas, the circumstances and the people to
help you take positive action.

## DAY 8

I received my money-tracker calendar today! I filled it in for the whole month with every bit of money that had come in. I'm choosing to focus on all the money coming in rather than focusing on what is going out.

Consistent action is vital and it's ok not to know exactly HOW I'm going to achieve my goal.

I'm beginning to accept and enjoy this as a game. I'm playing with the Universe. My job is to feel good, take consistent action, focus on what I want: ease and flow, money flowing to me, consistent income, clients coming in, new ideas and opportunities to grow my business and the completion of my book.

I am open to the infinite possibilities that my goal can be accomplished.

I decided last week to surround myself with money. I'm visual. I need to see money. So, I put 2 crisp £20 notes in a glass jar in my bedroom and that excites me whenever I see it (which is every single day!).

Then I put 2 x £20 notes in my purse and I've decided to always have money in my purse – facing forward, neatly presented to show my abundance and my respect for money. Whenever I open my purse, I see money.

3rd thing is that I did the Rhonda Byrne exercise of putting a post it note on a "dollar bill". I put mine on a brand new shiny £10 note.

The post it notes says "Thank you for all the money I've been given throughout my life"

Every day I hold that note and thank the universe for all the money I've ever received and all the money that is on its way to me.

Very powerful for raising my vibration and focusing on abundance.

Today I held a book and shut my eyes and allowed my fingers to trace over the embossed letters and the smooth cover and the hard spine and I pictured holding my book "PAID IN FULL".

**Call to Action:**

On a month to view calendar write each day you receive money. The denomination is irrelevant to the Universe, money is money so if it's 1p in the street – pick it up and declare "Thank you!! Money is everywhere, and I am receiving it".

Write down your income when it comes in, any benefits or gifts and money off vouchers and coupons. Play the game every day by setting an intention to seek out money from the gold-dust that's in the air!

Have money in your purse that you won't touch (my coach calls it her Warrior line). It might be a £10 or £20 note but that stays put. Also, find a nice clean jar for your bedroom and put the largest denomination note that you can in it, so you can clearly see it every day.

Have images of money and affirmative statements on your screensaver. Print out your credit card statements and bank statements, white out the balances and write the balances you want to see instead.

Make peace with your desires for money and abundance and be proud of yourself for your willingness to applying principles that will radically improve your mindset and your life.

# Harness Your Genius Power

Your genius power is your imagination. There is so much evidence to back up the powerful nature of your imagination and how it can support your goal achievement.

Successful men and women have known this for centuries – when you focus deliberately on what you want, and you visualise yourself already having it you are literally crafting it in to your reality.

Your subconscious mind does not know the difference between what is real and what is imagined. That may seem like a flaw, however it is one of the most powerful advantages we have in achieving whatever we want.

If you can flood your subconscious mind with an imagined experience until your subconscious believes that that experience has *actually* occurred, it changes your state of being.

Your state of being will resonate at the frequency of that which you've been focusing on and imagining, and by virtue of the powerful Law of Attraction, you will attract everything that is a match to your dominant vibration – the exact circumstances will manifest.

The key is to visualise the **result** that you want and infuse it with strong positive emotion.

When it comes to being debt free, what is going to be the most powerful evidence for you that you've achieved it?

Perhaps it will be the statements with £0 balance outstanding or the phone call to the creditor to joyfully request closure of the account.

Maybe it's the experience of gathering your loved ones for a lovely meal and seeing their faces as you explain, through joyful tears, that you are now debt free.

Practising visualisation every day is powerful for shifting your state of being. You feel excitement rather than stress. You feel positive and eager rather than negative and hopeless. You transition every day more and more into a state of receptivity to the possibilities around you and you attract more ideas and opportunities that will set you on your path.

As you begin to feel better day by day, you attract more to feel better about. It's a perpetual upward spiral! I've had debt my whole adult life. Many people have mortgage debt for most of their adult life but since I was 18, I have had credit card debt.

On the rare occasions that I had I paid it all off, somehow within a very short period I had accumulated it again. Being in debt had become so familiar to me that it was an uncomfortable comfort zone! I identified with it and was perpetuating it year on year.

In order to change my results, I had to change how I identified myself in the context of money and debt. This was where the power of visualisation was extremely valuable. Every day, sometimes multiple times a day I imagined how I'd feel being paid in full, I visualised this book being published, and I saw myself talking to people about how they can help themselves become free "just like I had!" Through repetition, I imprinted this experience onto my subconscious mind, like a memory.

This created a state change, over time in who I was being. The more I resonated as someone who did not have debt, the less I worried about it, and the more money and prosperity I attracted.

So, what did I experience when I imagined my desired outcome?

My whole body felt electric!! I was simply bursting with joy. I was crying happy tears as I saw myself opening the parcel that had just arrived and seeing my book inside "PAID IN FULL". As I turned the book over in my hands, I realised that I'm liberated and my purposeful journey to help other men and women feel free and amazing had begun in earnest.

In my imagination I fell to my knees and sobbed!! I sobbed tears of relief, pride, joy, elation, satisfaction and a sense of endings and new beginnings.

Then I saw myself getting ready for a special day and evening with Jeremy.     I gift wrapped my book, smiling to myself because god knows how I kept the book a secret from him for all this time!!

I'm normally rubbish at keeping exciting secrets to myself!! I'd prepared the works! Hotel booked, champagne on ice, new dress, new hairdo, nails, facial - I was scrubbed, buffed, moisturised and I felt a million dollars!! I was literally floating on air!

I was beyond excited to see Jeremys' face as he unwrapped this gift and the realisation of what it meant dawned on him. He can barely believe it!

My Coach, Hasnaa was with me for the entire journey and I saw myself writing her a letter (of course, there are tears!) of deep thanks and gratitude and explaining how she has helped me transform my life!

As I emerged from this powerful visualisation, my face wet with real tears of joy, I felt wonderful. I repeated this process almost every day – sometimes giving myself 30 – 45 minutes of immersion and other times just recalling some element of this end-result and focusing on it for 5 minutes.

This had the magical effect of having me believe ahead of time that I was debt free. I was creating my mental map of the future. This shifted my state of being and my vibration.

I stopped relying on credit cards to help me get by each month.

Whenever I needed or wanted something, I earned or attracted the money. I also saw my balances reducing with satisfaction and I diminished my stressful and negative thoughts because my whole perspective had changed.

**Call to Action:**

**Take 5-10 minutes every single day to change your state through the power of visualisation. Imagine the details of celebrating being paid in full. How do you feel? Who are you with? What are you wearing? Where are you and what are you doing?**

**Occasionally when you have more time, or create more time for yourself, give yourself the gift of a longer immersion into your visualisation. It not only feels utterly blissful, but you emerge from each experience changed at a fundamental cellular level – less the person you were who gets into debt, and more and more like the person in your visualisation! Paid in Full!**

# Recognising the significant internal shifts

I realised, 2 weeks into this process that I was beginning to create some significant internal shifts, that I was breaking some old negative patterns.

With the help of my coach Hasnaa, I identified an internal conflict that had kept me really stuck. The conflict was that I wanted to be clear of all debts and be Paid in Full and yet I was feeling gratitude for credit cards because they always 'bailed me out' and it was "easy money."

I needed to create a single point of focus, a single direction in which to face, that served me. I needed to shift my state of mind away from *"it's easy to look to credit"* to *"It's easy to make money"*

I broke down everything I knew about making money in my business, I went back to basics. This was to be my immediate plan of action.

I then replaced the gratitude I had for credit with gratitude for all the money I'd ever received. Hasnaa challenged me to list as many instances that I could recall of times when I really needed money, and I received it.

This was so empowering!

## DAY 13

"I had no money in the bank for groceries and just like that, a client showed up and paid me direct to my bank account -Thank you!

I decided not to go out for a meal because I couldn't justify the spending and Jeremy gave me a lovely card with £40 in it to pay for my dinner and a bottle of wine with my friends - thank you!


I was worried before Christmas how I'd manage and without saying a word Jeremy transferred £500 straight into my account – thank you!

I saved myself £170 a month right when I needed it when I rang my mortgage lenders and they gave me new and cheaper rates on my mortgages – thank you!

Money from my tenant arrives in my bank account every single month without fail right before my mortgage payment goes out – thank you!

I had a sleepless night back in the early days of my business and the very next day I created a programme and launched it and got 2 new clients – their monthly payment combined was the EXACT amount I needed to pay all my bills. Thank you!!

My latest launch of my group programme saw 5 women jump in – all within a 12 hour window – that money came right when I needed it – thank you!

The more I expressed gratitude for money received as opposed to money borrowed, the more money I attracted and the less I considered credit as a source of money! I was severing that tie, that belief that I was dependent on debt!

In the past I would not have thought twice, or rather I wouldn't have 'thought' at all, about using my credit cards to pay for gifts for loved ones. So, I recognised that I was breaking my old habits when it came to Jeremy's birthday. It wasn't easy, but I was making conscious decisions rather than acting unconsciously.

## DAY 14:

I burst into tears today as I had to speak to Jeremy about his Birthday coming up next month. I would love to be able to take care of EVERTHING and lay on an amazing surprise for him.

To book something awesome – all expenses paid.

However, a smart and savvy girl like me – in my current situation must be smarter than putting it on the credit card – which would have been my previous default behaviour. No! I had to talk to him about my concerns and be open to the truth that at this moment in time, it's not my priority financially.

It hurt my heart and I felt shame as I talked to him. The tears were so spontaneous. I feel shame telling someone "no", we can't do something because of a lack of money.

That was a deep-rooted emotion that emerged and explains a lot of my attitude in the past. I never said "no" because of money, because I didn't want to disappoint anyone. I didn't want to be disappointed for missing out myself and neither did I want to disappoint the person I was saying "no" to. I was a chronic people pleaser!!

## Self-acceptance

My initial plan when I made my decision to chronicle my journey was to keep this whole thing a secret from my loved ones. I wanted to first be Paid in Full and published, so then I could announce it to my loved ones as a *"Ta Daaaaa!! Suuurrrrprise!!!"* I imagined myself basking in their surprise and pride at what I'd accomplished all by myself.

The truth of the matter is that I'd more likely be handling their shock and sadness that I carried this burden alone and didn't trust them enough to share it with them!

It dawned on me 2 weeks into my journey that I was hiding. I wanted the glory without dealing with my own fears of rejection. This realisation was part of a second significant internal shift.

I had to trust my loved ones enough by trusting myself first.

I realised that this was a massive part of the puzzle that was missing in my quest for the truth that comes with acknowledging 'what is'. I realised that the shame of my debt was pervading every cell of my body and was manifesting as secrecy.

I was hiding my situation from my loved ones and that was reinforcing my fear of rejection and shame. I was also lying, to myself and my partner, Jeremy, who shared my life with me but had no idea what I was going through.

This was one of the scariest moments for me. I'd tried to talk to Jeremy in the past but bottled it. I imagined judgement and criticism and awful rejection – that I wouldn't be lovable anymore because I'm an unlovable screw up, a loser.

I know now that that was simply my projection of how I saw myself.

I needed to release the shame and to forgive and accept myself. And one of the biggest steps to achieving that was to tell Jeremy the whole truth.

This realisation actually emerged by accident as I was self-coaching through this powerful journaling process!

## DAY 15

I am loving reading Napoleon Hill's "Think and Grow Rich" and as I read this morning, yet more nuggets of wisdom dropped in.

Hill writes "I realise that the dominating thoughts of my mind will eventually reproduce themselves in outward physical action and gradually transform themselves into physical reality..."

As I read this, what stood out more than ever before was the line "reproduce themselves in outward physical action..." which is all about taking the action that needs to be taken.

Which means to respond with action to the inspired thoughts and new ideas that are going to come. These are the thoughts and ideas that attract more matching thoughts and ideas until a plan has hatched.

Just as Hill says "...any desire that I persistently hold in my mind will eventually seek expression through some practical means of attaining the object back of it..." The way I interpret that is Hill is saying to hold the thought persistently and get really practiced at listening to oneself. To listen and observe the divine downloads and then ACT on them.

Which really tells me that whilst I have spent years telling myself that I don't know how to make multiple 6-figures in my business and that I can't imagine it for myself – that's exactly what has been my block.

If I imagined myself and held on persistently to the idea of making multiple 6 figures, then I'm going to attract the ideas and opportunities to make that happen.

Just like I have always done in most other areas of my life! I've always achieved what I've set out to achieve and yet the subject of money and debt has been the fly in the ointment!

It's important to listen to myself and the things I am telling myself over and over – there is so much unconsciousness here. Even though I think I'm being conscious

When I really think about it, I say things all the time that don't serve me! I say: "I can't remember, I have a terrible memory" all the time! Duh! I say: "I can't get my words out" quite often too!!

Something I do that is limiting me is that I hide my "Paid in full" statements and my income tracking calendar from Jeremy! I don't' share any of my "manifesting" and mindset processes with him.

Why?

Because I have some shame around the activities I'm doing. I feel embarrassed to be using vision boards and affirmations

Why?

Because I think Jeremy will think I'm silly or the kids will be cynical...yes, I think they'll judge me as being a dreamer and I feel ashamed.

What is the vibration that I'm vibrating at when I feel shame? Holy Fuck. I've just googled "Human vibration chart" and Shame is at the bottom as the lowest and most contracted vibration.

I need to get rid of this shame!!

How can I feel no shame around my activities – my mindset work; my daily affirmations and vision boards?

How about I start re-writing that story right now?

I no longer have shame around my debt – I accept myself and the choices I made in the past fully. I am celebrating conscious awareness and a desire to grow through this. I am open to utilising all the tools and resources at my disposal to write a new story.

I stopped writing my journal in that moment of realisation, that I was hiding, I knew that I needed to confront my shame with Jeremy. I was sat at my dining table with all my paper work and Jeremy was on his lap- top in the lounge. I asked him to come over.

## DAY 16:

What an emotional day yesterday was! Confronting my shame head on and recognising it fully. I was of course aware of the shame, but I wasn't doing anything about it – I was perpetuating the lie that was causing the shame. The lie was "with this debt I'm not worthy". I believed that I risked rejection from the people who love me. And by keeping it a secret and hiding the amount from Jeremy I was keeping the shame very much a part of the whole story.

I wrote this on my statements:

I accept myself and the choices I made in the past fully without blame, shame or guilt. I am celebrating conscious awareness and a desire to grow through this. I am open to utilising all the tools and resources at my disposal to write a new story. I am loved and supported no matter what.

I then called Jeremy over to engage in a conversation. I started rambling and going around the houses with tears in my eyes explaining that I feel so much shame around money and that it's not serving me and how I want to be free of the shame and as we talked about the situation I am in, he gently asked "how much is it?" ...

I couldn't even say it out loud! I broke it down as if to somehow lessen it..." well I owe this much (as I wrote £10,000) to mum and then...around this (as I wrote £37,000) on my credit cards and overdraft"

Then we had an open conversation. He came over to my side of the table to take a look at the paper work around me and he asked me some questions about what is on the overdraft and how many credit cards do I have and as we talked, I just got more matter of fact about it all and something shifted.

Later I felt like I could breathe freely without the usual lump in my solar plexus that I've been carrying for almost 18 months.

First, we have to be honest with ourselves and experience the pain and then the empowerment of the truth...

And then we have to share the truth with those who matter most to us.

As I write this, I'm on the beginning of my exciting journey and I'm dealing with all the gremlins along the way – taking every day as it comes and focusing on income, my book, helping millions of people become debt free and learning to become a new person without the identity of debt.

I wrote this declaration out on all my credit card statements:

"I no longer have shame around my debt – I accept myself and the choices I made in the past fully. I am celebrating conscious awareness and a desire to grow through this. I am open to utilising all the tools and resources at my disposal to write a new story"

I know how fortunate I am, and that Jeremys' support and love has given me strength. However, I feel it's important to add that no matter what his reaction, I still needed to forgive and accept myself and this was a part of that. Remembering that debt has no meaning but the meaning we attach to it, applies to everyone!

This was one of the most significant moments of this entire journey.

## DAY 18

Debt is just debt. It only has meaning based on the meaning we attach to debt. I have spent so long pushing at it, hating myself for it, rejecting myself because I felt such shame around it that I feared rejection from others.

As I write this the stark realisation of how truly hard on myself, I have been for so many years is so sad and so unnecessary. And I perpetuated more debt by coming from that place of self-hatred and shame because I believed that the "next purchase" of personal development would be the golden ticket to paying it off – ironically.

But also, I held it in my focus (and Law of Attraction gave me more of what I focused on) and not only that – I rejected myself and therefore couldn't show up authentically in my business.

I rejected myself and others rejected me too. So, I didn't make money and therefore ploughed through what savings I had and had to borrow more just to cover the bills.

So, as I release all shame and I repeat – "I accept myself and the choices I made in the past fully – without blame, shame or guilt. I am celebrating conscious awareness and my desire to grow through this…I am loved and supported no matter what…" I am finding myself feeling so much kinder to myself and I am receiving more acceptance and kindness in return. In the form of my clients coming in and Jeremy giving me so much love and acceptance and support.

Whilst I was the subject of my own "experiment" and in the moment of it all, 18 days felt like a long time, but as I sit here reflecting and writing it's very clear to me how quickly things can change when we really apply ourselves.

In less than 3 weeks I was breaking through some of my most destructive patterns of thought and behaviour; making conscious decisions, rather than acting from default and beginning to show myself compassion and self-acceptance. This is huge and leads me perfectly into the next subject of values.

# Your Valuable Values

Our values act like a compass for our best life. They represent what is most important to us, in effect, what is valuable to us.

Moment to moment, when you're happy and appreciating life, you can put money on it's because some, or all, of your highest values are being met.

Equally when you're experiencing dissatisfaction and a lack of joy, it's because your values are being compromised or you're living out of alignment with your highest values.

Part of my work with my clients is helping them get clarity on their life purpose. I take them through a process, a kind of interview style guided conversation during which we traverse their life-story and plot their journey. People's stories fascinate and delight me!

They reveal everything about who they are at their core, what they're truly passionate about and what they're strengths and unique gifts

97

are. It's a wonderful enlightening process and brings so much clarity to the individual.

As part of this process we discuss values.

As the client shares their times of struggle when they faced challenges or conflict, those darker periods they've endured and ultimately overcome, the patterns emerge with crystal clarity. They experienced the pain of certain situations more acutely when their core values were being compromised, or even crushed.

If one of your highest values is connection for example, and you found yourself joining a new company or moving to a new city in which you didn't know anyone, you're likely to feel quite unhappy until you'd got to know people and made some friends with whom to connect.

I wouldn't feel remotely unhappy in this situation because connection isn't one of my highest values. But put me in a situation where I'm dependent on other people, then I'll feel constricted and miserable because I value independence!

Therefore, knowing your values and having them steer your decisions is critical to feeling happy, raising your vibration and feeling congruent mind, body and soul.

As you're understanding what and why things feel good to you, as well as why and what makes you feel bad you can make more empowered choices for yourself.

And again, the more time you spend feeling good and in a state of satisfaction and happiness, you'll attract to you more to feel good about and thus propel you on your upward trajectory away from thoughts of fear, lack and scarcity and into abundance and joy.

There are many techniques to help you get clear on your values but one way that I love is this:

Think of 5 memories of when you were full of joy and contentment, when you just felt so darn good – whether you were belly laughing or in extreme peace and serenity - just bring them to mind.

Write a detailed description of each scenario. Who you were with? What you were doing? What made it so utterly blissful, exciting, joyful for you? What was the essence of the memory that stands out the most for you?

Reflect on each memory and how good you felt. This activity alone is powerful for raising your vibration and attracting more to feel good about!

Notice all the connections, the common themes or factors that link some, or all of the scenarios that you've written about.

Here's mine by way of example.

1) *October 2014 I was driving on the motorway in my new car on my way to a personal development seminar or coaching school weekend event (I can't remember exactly because I went to so many seminars and trainings in my first 2 years of business!) These events meant more to me because I enjoyed the added bonus of seeing my mum and her husband, Paul. They'd accommodate me for the weekend because the events were always in or around London, where they lived. On this memorable occasion, as I was driving, I became overwhelmed with a deep sense of joy and tears streamed down my cheeks and I was laughing at the same time! Yes, I was alone in the car! I just knew in that moment, that I was on my purposeful path in my new business.*

2) *November 2016, I went to Portugal with my dearest friends Jen and Sofia. The three of us got together for a business planning retreat. We talked and talked for 3 days solid about "deep shit", the meaning of life and our big why's. We coached one another, we discussed our businesses and we laughed. Boy did we laugh. It felt magical.*

3) *December 2016, Jeremy and I flew to Boston for 5 days, so I could attend a 3 day business retreat with my coach, Becky. Becky had arranged for Jack Canfield to spend a day with us, sharing his success principles with us. There were only 10 of us in that room so it was intimate and powerful.*

4) *Climbing. I've completed several challenging walks including the National 3 Peaks and I absolutely love it! In 2017 Jeremy, his son and I climbed the 3 peaks in England as part of a group fundraising. I love being in nature and taking in the expansive views, I love the physical challenge and I get such a kick out of the sense of achievement and accomplishment at the end!*

*Plus, when you're walking together*
*for such long distances there's a*
*wonderful camaraderie and banter.*

5) *Post marriage separation, I found myself in*
*a house that was by all accounts,*
*uninhabitable (filthy carpets and walls, an*
*empty kitchen with just a sink in it that*
*spewed out brown water; a dining room*
*ceiling that collapsed due to the persistent*
*leaking toilet above...) I was 38 and hadn't*
*changed so much as a lightbulb in 18 years!*
*My ex-husband had managed everything*
*when it came to home maintenance, so I felt*
*powerless in my ignorance. August 2013*
*when I moved into this new property, I had*
*to take massive action. It was*
*overwhelming and frightening. I spent a*
*few days in bewilderment but then it was*
*like a flame inside of me started to flicker to*
*life. I became a Do-It-Yourself home*
*maintenance fiend!! I asked my colleagues*
*questions, I watched how-to videos on*
*YouTube, I hung out in the aisles of B&Q!*
*I went to work every day in my suit and*
*then by night I was in my scruffs, up and*
*down ladders, stripping, sanding, painting,*
*fixing – sometimes I didn't make it to bed. I*
*worked through the night. I loved it!! I*
*listened to music all night and worked.*

*Some days I went to my day job with hands that were cut and sore to the point that it hurt to hold a pen! But I felt amazing! I loved seeing the progress and I loved even more feeling my own sense of self-worth growing. Within a few months, I had created a beautiful and colourful home for me and my children. People commented that they felt the love when they entered. My home had become my metaphor that I hold on to when I feel like I'm buckling under a challenge. If I can do that, I can do anything!*

Thank you for indulging me there for a moment! I thoroughly enjoyed this exercise for myself and I encourage you to give it a go.

The themes that stood out for me as being connecting themes are independence, hanging out with like-minded people and have meaningful conversations; personal development and learning; taking action, accomplishment and recognition.

I found this exercise exhilarating because whilst I thought I knew my values, this revealed with such crystal clarity new values that immediately made perfect sense to me. Understanding what makes me happy and why I get so frustrated at times means that I can be more conscious and deliberate in the choices I make day to day with the deliberate intention of feeling more in flow and more joyful.

# Your Emotional Guidance System

With each passing day, as I trained myself into increased conscious awareness of my thoughts and feelings, I gained more clarity.

As I spent time in daily disciplines of gratitude practice, visualisation and journaling (more on journaling later) I began to experience more compassion for myself. I realised how miserable I had been for so many years, how hard and self-critical I was and how this state of being was not serving me at all.

Nothing comes of beating yourself up for your past choices and decisions. Seriously, nothing! There is no virtue to be found in guilt and shame, in putting yourself down or arguing in favour of your limitations.

What emerged day by day was a deepening appreciation and trust in my emotional guidance system in relation to my decisions around what action to take to clear my debt.

105

Now I've talked already about how important it is to train your focus in order to feel good more of the time, as Abraham Hicks calls it thinking more "better feelings thoughts" and I've touched on your values as being a compass for your decision making.

Now I want to share how I discovered how to use my emotional guidance system for making my debt-repayment decisions. I had 5 credit cards with balances ranging from less than £1k right up to £18k; I had a personal loan of £10k from my mum and I had an expensive overdraft of £3.5k.

In the beginning I focused on repaying the 2 smaller balances. I wanted the sense of achievement – the quick wins that would give me cause to celebrate earlier on. This is called the "snowball method" when you pay off the debts in order of balance, focusing on the smaller balances first whilst paying the minimum payments required to the larger balances.

This is irrespective of interest rates and to whom the money is owed.

The "avalanche method" of debt repayment considers the most expensive debt as being the priority. The avalanche method is probably the most sensible and 'savvy' method however, since I was working on overcoming years of conditioning in seeming opposition to 'sensible and savvy' I needed to find a way that worked for me!

Within 3 weeks I had cleared my 2 smallest balances and I was euphoric! I loved the quick wins and felt energised and encouraged by the progress.

What followed was a dilemma that introduced me to an alternative approach to deciding which debt to focus on next.

After the 2 smallest balances were cleared, I had an expensive overdraft of £3500 and a 0% credit card of the same amount.  It seemed obvious. I had to pay off my overdraft and get myself into a credit position in my current account.

Suddenly I experienced fear. I literally felt the blood drain from my face as I contemplated not having an overdraft facility. I knew that once I had cleared the balance, I also had to remove the facility otherwise I feared I wouldn't ever be fully free. The intensity of my emotion was momentarily overwhelming and caught me off guard.

At first, I considered leaving the overdraft alone and repaying the credit card, but I quickly realised that if I did this, I was letting fear dictate my decision for me. Also, there was another important issue that I hadn't previously considered or realised was important. I didn't want to focus on the 0% credit card because I felt no emotion around it. I couldn't seem to stoke up any of that vital excitement around paying it off.

Why? As strange as it seems to say this now, I had no emotional attachment to that credit card or what the balance represented. It was the most recent card I'd acquired, and I had applied for it specifically to get the benefit of a 0% balance transfer. I felt as though I didn't have any 'history' with this card!

This got me thinking about the emotional attachments I had, in relation to each of the debtors and what the debts represented. I realised that this was going to be an important factor in deciding the order of repayment.

So, my emotional guidance system became my debt repayment guidance system!

I analysed each of the debt in turn and checked in with my emotional guidance system, asking myself "How does this debt make me feel? What emotions are coming up when I think about this particular debt and my ability to repay it?"

The largest credit card balance and my overdraft carried the strongest negative emotions – one because the balance felt insurmountable and the other because I believed I couldn't manage financially without it!

The debt that unearthed some surprising emotions was the money I owed to my mum. I cried when she offered me the loan to help me buy my garden-office from which to operate my business. I was, and always continue to be, blown away by her total belief and faith in me! Whilst I was very aware of this debt and I frequently imagined the elation and joy I'd feel paying it back in full, I assumed that this would be the last one I repaid. My mum never mentioned it and didn't set any timescales for repayment, and there was no interest rate to worry about.

However, when I checked in with my emotional guidance system, I recognised that this debt was actually causing me some internal conflict.

As much as it was lent to me in good faith, I was harbouring guilt. One minute I'd be cheerfully telling mum about my fun long weekend away and then next minute I'd feel a pang of guilt "If I can afford to go away, I can afford to repay mum". If I shared successes and new clients with mum, she'd be nothing but happy for me, but I'd wind up feeling bad with thoughts of "If I'm doing so great, why aren't I repaying mum?"

I recognised that I needed to challenge some of my beliefs and I felt ready to do so. I decided that the overdraft was going to be next and that really had nothing to do with it being the most expensive, rather what it represented. If I could get myself into a credit position, I would be giving myself a new and empowering story that I am a good money manager. It means finally overcoming the bogus belief that I can't manage without an overdraft facility. Then from that more empowered state I could make a new decision based on which to pay off next.

## DAY 19

I have been practising the snowball technique for clearing debt which isn't about clearing the most expensive one first

– it's about getting the motivation and the enjoyment from clearing the smaller ones and reducing the number of little balances. That I like!

So next I'm going to employ a slightly different tactic. I think...well, I'm still pondering, I have my £3500 overdraft which is very expensive. It's costing me about £30 per month in interest – and I IMAGINE that I can't manage without it (mmm)...and I have my card that Jeremy holds for me with about £3400.

But I never think about that one, perhaps because Jeremy holds onto it and I don't see it physically, it's easy to forget and never think about.

I don't have too much emotion around that – plus its 0%. I also have my Bank of Scotland which costs me 0% and has about £11500 on it and I don't have much emotion around that. THEN there's my Barclaycard at £18k. Now I seem to have a lot of emotion swirling around that one.

So, my thoughts are – the two that carry emotion ought to be looked at first. There's my overdraft that I seem to think I can't manage without or my Barclaycard which is big enough to currently feel insurmountable.

Both emotions, dependent or insurmountable, feel bad and are not serving me. Something deep inside me wants to challenge myself and knock the overdraft on the head once and for all. To get into credit.

Oh yessssss!!! That actually feels really good! To have a bank account that lives in credit feels way healthier to me. And is greater evidence of my love for myself that I easily manage my money!!

Yes, that's IT!! I'm still giving myself the message that I'm a poor money manager and that money isn't flowing to me by my reluctance to get into CREDIT and STAY THERE.

Nice bit of self- coaching there!!! I'm going to say bye-bye to the Halifax card this week...and then I'm going to pay off my overdraft. Oh! My heart is singing!!!

My new affirmations: I live in credit! I love living in credit. I always have more than enough money in my bank account to cover all my outgoings and expenses. I love having more than enough money in my bank and seeing it grow.

I am an excellent money manager and I love myself truly!

## DAY 22

Wow Wow Wow! Thank you thank you thank you – I have been affirming my accounts overflowing with money and this morning I realised that I sent too much to pay off the Halifax so not only am I PAID IN FULL with the Halifax– but my account is overflowing! Nice!

I intend to close this down today.

I've been starting to dilute the impact of my money tracker calendar recently because I've been adding lots of extra's for which I'm grateful like meals paid for. I feel like that dilutes the impact of the income received so from now on, I'm going to stick to journaling my gratitude and use the calendar simply for money received.

One important realisation this weekend was around the importance of our choice of words.

The brain thinks in pictures, so it's been the difference that has made the difference to have visual representations of what I want.

It's been so powerful to have the credit card statements with PAID IN FULL written on them. Also, now as I focus on my overdraft – I realise the importance of finding the right words that truly resonate.

I want words that evoke an immediate emotional response. For example, as I was playing around with words of affirmation for my overdraft I hit on "my bank account is overflowing with money". I could physically feel those words in my chest and my heart and they instantly uplifted my spirits. I pictured money spilling over the sides of my bank account. I felt truly abundant.

So now the next important step here is to get a current account statement and edit it so that it's in credit. That is my next big move.

I'm affirming "I am an excellent money manager!"

I do feel nervous right now about my ability to clear my overdraft permanently but I'm taking this as the perfect indication that this is the work on myself that needs to happen.

## DAY 23

I found a bank statement and wrote "OVERFLOWING" in red on it and pinned it next to my Barclaycard and Bank of Scotland statements that have "PAID IN FULL" emblazoned across them. They look good and they feel great!

Yesterday I had an emotional and affirming experience.

I'm a member of a close-knit community of female entrepreneurs all part of a year-long mentoring programme with my business coach Michelle. On my accountability form I shared my win –

paying off my 2$^{nd}$ credit card. Michelle privately messaged me to congratulate me and she asked me to share this big win with the other ladies as it's "inspirational."

So, I went straight into the group and did a live-stream to share how I had a love hate relationship with debt – I hate it, but it loves me! I told the group about my win and I told them about this book.

I was overwhelmed with emotion by the response I received. Women telling me how strong in my vulnerability I am and how inspiring I am! Women telling me how they could relate to the debt situation and the emotions around it. I was heartened and uplifted by that response. Every now and again, I think "oh this book is a silly idea" and I get scared, so this was just what I needed right now!

I'm excited and this has put a little renewed energy in to the whole process. That's important, the renewed energy.

## DAY 24

As soon as I made my decision to repay my overdraft and get into a credit position, I had the simple idea to offer my group coaching programme to 10 people for £600 each.

I'm really believing now that I can easily make the money – that money comes easily. I'm beginning to truly embrace that. There is a little part of me – at the back of my mind – that still sees only 2 or 3 people coming in to something I promote rather than the 10 I want.

There's a part of me that doesn't believe that it will have maximum capacity.

I need to re-write that story really damn quickly. In the past I've worked so hard on promoting launches and whilst I've loved getting people in, I've never achieved my goal. I want 10 people in, I'm lucky to get 5! Every single time! So, now I have a story inside me that says "It's hard to fill a group programme"

But that's me gauging my future performance on my past performance. Every day is a new opportunity to create a new outcome, a new future. The future hasn't happened yet, so I can do something different. And it all begins with thinking different thoughts.

#1 The past is NOT an indication of future results

#2 You'll always get what you always got if you always do what you always did – so DO SOMETHING DIFFERENT!!

#3 Create affirmations to reframe and re-train the mind to think "fully booked"

#4 Research "sell out launches" for some ideas

#5 Focus on the outcome and be crystal clear i.e. state a number and then focus on that.

## DAY 25

I'm reading Napoleon Hill's "Think and Grow Rich" again. I've read it perhaps 3 times before and certainly I've read isolated chapters many times in the past, but I have to say that reading it this time, I have a depth of understanding that was missing before.

Previously, I read it thinking "Oh! That's nice" and "Wow! I'm inspired!" but so much was missing.

I followed the instructions and I'd write my definite chief aim, for example "to have £220k (or whatever) to be debt and mortgage free" and I focused on it for a few days maybe even weeks, but it lacked the burning desire. I don't think I truly believed it and I didn't have a sense of purpose around it.

What is different this time is the associated purpose to becoming Paid in Full. I have a strong attachment to the fact that my purpose is to help others focus on the "right" things, so they can truly transform their lives. I hear myself saying a lot "Well, yes, you can tell that story...or you can change it" both to myself and to my clients when the focus is negative and non-serving.

I also had some huge breakthrough realisations and enjoyed noticing some serendipities. This week the memory of my A-level biology re-sit came to mind, seemingly out of the blue. I had a deep urge to share the story, but I didn't know why.

I felt slightly silly, but I went live in my Facebook group and I told the tale of the lady who showed up to help me at the 11th hour, when I'd all but lost hope.

{In brief, early 2010, when I worked for the building society, a lady came to me to discuss her mortgage repayments, she had hit on hard times. She told me she was looking for jobs in schools. A week later my children brought home a school newsletter that included a notice seeking supervisory staff.

I immediately thought of this lady and although we'd only met the once, I posted her the school newsletter with a note saying "I saw this and thought of you". I didn't hear anything from her again. 2 years later, I went to sit my biology exam and this same lady was an invigilator!

Although we'd only met that one time 2 years earlier, we instantly recognised one another, and our brief exchange was warm and friendly. She told me how grateful she was to me and how she'd got a new job quickly after our meeting. She was surprised to see me, a building society manager at an A 'level biology exam!

I confided in her that I was studying to pursue a new career in midwifery.

When my exam results came through, I discovered that I had to do a re-sit 6 months later. I was gutted but determined.

On the night before my re-sit, the UK was hit by the worst snow storms in decades! The roads were grid-locked! I left my home for the exam with plenty of hours to spare but the journey was hazardous. A 20-minute journey took over 2 hours and I was about a mile away from the exam centre with literally minutes to go.

I was crying with stress! I decided to pull over, abandon the car and RUN!!! I ran and ran as fast as it was possible in the blizzard and the thick fresh snow underfoot. As I ran up to the front door of the building, I crashed into it! It was locked! It was exactly 9am and the exam started at 9am.

Suddenly the same lady came tearing down the corridor, unlocked the door and hurried me in. She said "I knew you'd be here. I saw your name on my list and I knew you wouldn't miss it. I've been waiting for you!!"

By 9.01am I was sat in the exam. I passed}

As I reached the end of my Facebook live-stream, I started to sum it up by saying "so there you go, you do good deeds and good deeds come back to you blah blah blah..." Suddenly, the truth of the story emerged clearly in my mind.

The real point of that experience is that most people give up at the first signs of defeat...as soon as things start to appear hopeless ... when, the truth is, it's never the end until it's over!

You see, I ran and ran to the exam even though I knew that I'd missed the door, I knew I was too late, but I just kept running and the lady was waiting for me...and she helped me sit the exam and I passed!

That led me to recall the events of my last group programme launch, when I signed up my 5 clients all in the final 12 hours before the doors closed! I'd been promoting it for weeks and nobody had expressed any interest! At the point when most people would have given up (those last 24 hours), I did the opposite, I "UP-ed" my activity! I just believed that it wasn't done until it was done!

Suddenly reading Hills' chapter - "3 Feet from Gold" – the sentiment makes perfect sense to me – it all makes perfect sense that this is what I was supposed to learn. Holy shit!

I was supposed to read that! I received that memory and at first, I didn't know why. Why I had an urge to share the story and what was its' relevance to anything?

I see it now!! It's the message to keep going! To never give up because you never know when you're 3 feet from gold!

Adversity, pain, facing defeat is often what connects us to our higher self – I know I've experienced it in my life many times. Times when I've been close to giving up but I didn't, by holding on and not giving up I tapped into my other self – that other self that exists within all of us like the bird in the egg or the oak tree in the acorn.

# Navigating the Rocks in the Road

Starting any new endeavor is exciting. You feel fresh and full of expectancy and hope. Taking action feels really good and you declare "This is it! I'm on my way!!"

Any fears you may have felt becomes excitement and you may even experience some "beginners' luck" when that initial excitement and energy is so profound and tangible that you get a quick early "win".

It's inevitable considering the law of attraction being at play with you, supporting you and loving you and responding to your powerful vibration.

Your energy is like a power surge and you feel unstoppable…well, at least you do for a few weeks.

Ever tried quitting smoking, embarking on a new diet and fitness regime or for that matter anything that involves change?

Before long the resolve starts to waiver and in a moment of weakness you slip back into the old habit – perhaps even justifying it to yourself as a reward "I've been good all week, one biscuit won't hurt" or "I'll use my credit card for that – just this one last time…"

Or the 'gremlins' start chattering in your mind: *Who do you think you are? That's enough now – you've entertained us for long enough – time to go back to how you were! You can't do this. You're not good enough. See? I told you, you wouldn't last…"*

What makes change so hard, after such a promising beginning? Why do we fall off the wagon – whether it's quitting smoking, losing weight, finishing the course of study, sticking to a schedule or in the context of this book, staying on track with becoming "Paid in Full"?

It pretty much boils down to the same thing.

The stories we tell ourselves, about ourselves! I'm talking about self- perception – who we believe ourselves to be and what we believe is possible for us.

Unfortunately, much of our stories and beliefs are beneath the surface of our conscious awareness. We don't know what we don't know. It's said that 90% of our behaviours are being driven by subconscious habits of thought. These subconscious habits of thought become beliefs that dominate our perspective.

We're acting from conditioning rather than conscious awareness! We're unaware of our dominant focus because it's become a state of being.

This conditioned state of being originates from childhood. From erroneous beliefs passed down from our immediate family, teachers, peers and community. It's come from the stories we told ourselves, about ourselves as children, as we navigated our way through life and made sense of our experiences.

Stories and beliefs such as "I'm not good / worthy / deserving / smart / pretty / slim / you fill in the blank – enough"

Our brains then naturally sought evidence that reinforced those beliefs and stories because they kept us safe, they were familiar.

And so, we learn to play small, believing that we're only as good as what our experience is reflecting back to us.

When we try to exert change in any area of our life, whether it's to breakthrough a pattern to become debt free or to lose weight, we have a strong internal force that is pulling us back. The internal force is almighty against any conscious exertion of effort for a very simple reason:

It's designed to keep us safe, and alive.

Our brains are built for survival, to keep us alive. Anything that threatens our survival switches on our primal instinct to pull back, stay safe, hide. It's your primitive lizard brain that is responsible for your fight/ flight responses that is kicking up a chemical storm and you begin to feel bad.

Logically, you may be thinking – but this is crazy – the smoking is killing me. The extra pounds are dangerous to my heart and my well-being. I want to become debt free – why is that a threat to my survival for crying out loud?!

Its' not logical.

However, the truth is, we're acting on conditioned, pre-programmed habits of thought that started in childhood, habits of thought that are both inaccurate and limited.

As children we didn't know how to process many of our experiences – especially the experiences that were upsetting or traumatic in some way whether that was being teased in the playground, told off by your mum or being too young to understand your parents' divorce.

As children we try to make sense of these experiences and the intense feelings we're having, and we believe it somehow must be about us. We think "there must be something wrong with me".

So, we develop beliefs about not being good enough, about being undeserving or unworthy. We become fearful of rejection or ridicule.

We adopt identities that determine our behaviours, and our behaviours bring about experiences that reinforce those identities until it's just a part of who we are.

When we think a thought for long enough and we think a thought persistently enough, it becomes a belief. The belief becomes a part of our identity, it becomes ingrained until we're no longer aware of it as a just a thought we once had, instead we refer to it as our personality or character.

# "Beliefs are just thoughts you keep thinking"

**Abraham Hicks**

But these unconscious habitual beliefs get stirred when we begin to exert change.

Change has consequences, it upsets the apple cart, rocks the boat. It means identifying yourself in a different way and it carries the potential for judgement, criticism and rejection from those who know and love us as we are.

Think about it this way, you have your circle of friends and family. People around with whom you feel safe and accepted and comfortable. Everything is familiar and habitual and safe because you've made it so.

That doesn't necessarily imply happiness, it simply means that you have a sense of safety that keeps your fear responses quiet and dormant.

But then you decide you want to change. You want to grow and do something different.

That threatens your internal status quo because it implies risk. You risk judgement from your family, your tribe. Maybe they'll reject you. To our primitive brain, rejection and being exiled from our tribe meant certain death. Better to stay the same and remain accepted and safe!

So as much as we want change and we know logically that the changes are for our greater good, our subconscious mind doesn't know this and so we will engage in self-sabotage.

I had my most significant breakthroughs during this part of my journey – as my self-sabotaging behaviours started to show up. It wasn't easy, but I knew that I had a choice. I could do what I've always done which was to back down, give up and feel hopeless again without ever really knowing what happened…

…OR I could face the saboteurs head on.

It's said that our biggest personal growth occurs during our greatest challenges and so as you take this journey, I want to reassure you that as you navigate the saboteurs, firstly you're armed with this information which is super powerful and secondly, it's so worth staying the course!

I do assert that this process for me has been a spiritual journey because in undertaking it, I've come to recognise my subconscious patterns of thought that have created my reality and therefore I'm able to interpret my results in any area of my life with more clarity, ease and precision.

I have become enlightened to my true power to create my own reality. It's the same for everyone. It's the same for you.

As you survey your results in any area of your life from this new perspective (of being a powerful creator of your own reality) you can determine what thought patterns you're running. The truth is that your external reality reflects your inner world and you have control over how you experience anything and everything in your life.

As you navigate your way through the rocks in the road along this journey, my desire is to help you raise your self-awareness, to identify your saboteurs and to recognise that you have ultimate creative control over your reality.

## DAY 27

Missed morning 26 and 27

It's the NIGHT of day 27...I have missed my gratitude journaling and my usual writing and visualising routine!! Be warned!! These activities are my NON-Negotiables.

Yesterday I spent my usual mindset work time "chasing" down old potential leads – people that I realise now would have hired me already if they were going to.

**I was forcing things instead of feeling into some ease and flow. So of course, they said "no".**

I also felt scattered and overwhelmed. This morning I got into a bit of a self-doubting state as one of my booked discovery calls cancelled...so I began to think, or rather 'overthink'!

I began to think that what I'm doing isn't working.

The anxiety was several things – the old story of "what if only a couple of people buy into my group coaching programme, then they'll see that I'm not as popular as they think, and they'll wonder if I'm the real deal"

And the second thing is that I don't want Jeremy to think I'm some kind of dreamer!

I'm seeing (imagining) a slight disbelief or dare I say 'sympathy' as I chase my next £6k goal. (This is the goal to clear my overdraft and get into a healthy credit position) Interesting!! Is this a reflection of my lack of belief in myself? Uh Oh!!

I recognised in myself that I was starting to try to control how things were going to pan out, rather than trusting the process.

To this end it was a wonderful joy that I had found myself at a Playful Improvisations workshop for today. I was so pleased to be attending this to take my mind off everything for the time being and really have some fun and laughter.

The workshop was amazing – I had an absolute ball and I was just so in the moment. Then when I got home, I hopped on a discovery call and with total ease and zero anxiety I signed a new client. She paid instantly, without any hesitation. That felt amazing and I haven't stopped celebrating since!!!

# Releasing Resistance

If you're reading this and you've come this far then congratulations, high fives and chest bumps!!

So many people buy books with all good intentions but never get beyond the first few pages! But not you!! You're determined and focused and beyond ready to experience the peace of mind and the joy that comes from being Paid in full.

Let me begin this section by telling you that this journey isn't about will- power, exertion and "pushing through" your fears and sub-conscious blocks, 'feel the fear and do it anyway' style.

It's about asking intelligent questions, tuning into your feelings and emotions and interpreting your moment to moment experiences.

It's about slowing down, listening, observing and enjoying those bittersweet A-

Ha insights that will make jelly of your legs (in a really good way!)

First, an explanation of what I mean by resistance. Resistance is the opposite of receiving.

When I think about receiving, I think of being open and expectant. Open minded and open-hearted, emitting a vibration that is smooth and free flowing. The positive out flow of energy is a gentle, yet powerful, undulating frequency that is easy and clear in intention.

Resistance on the other hand is like rapid jerky high frequency static. It's noisy and confusing. It blocks the flow of energy. It keeps you fenced in and perpetuating your current 'reality' because you can't see beyond the what is-ness of your experience.

Resistance is the thoughts, feelings and behaviours that holds you apart from what you want. Negative stinking thinking, feelings of fear and anxiety, procrastination, overwhelm and even working to the brink of burn out are all forms of resistance.

Resistance has a vibration that is counter to the free-flowing vibration of receiving.

I said earlier that your job is to feel good! That's it!

When you feel good more of the time, you attract more to feel good about! When you acknowledge and appreciate those experiences, you magnetise even more!

When you find yourself experiencing a negative experience you automatically have a thought along the lines of "I don't want this" and in that moment you have more clarity on what you **do** want.

For example, if you're in an argument with your spouse, you emit a desire for more harmony; If you receive an unexpected bill, you emit a desire for more money; If you have an injury or illness, you emit a desire for wellness and good health

Abraham Hicks calls these emissions "rockets of desire". These rockets fire out in to the Universe and the Universe is responding to you. Think of them as vibrational requests that once made has the Universe busy gathering together all of the necessary co-operative components to create the physical manifestation.

What stops your desires manifesting into your reality is, again, your choice of focus. You know you want harmony with your spouse, more money for your bills and improved health because the nature of your current reality has clarified that for you. But rather than focusing on those positive desires you stay simmering over the argument or worrying about the bill or talking about your injury or illness to whomever will listen.

You keep the negative experience 'active' in your vibration. You unwittingly introduce resistance.

Feeling good means holding fast to the feelings that the desire, the preferred state evokes, and riding the high vibe frequency of expectation and excitement. It means being open-minded and open-hearted in order to receive the inspired ideas, opportunities and possibilities that start showing up in response to your energy.

But instead of doing that, within a few precious moments, the mind starts chattering! "*I want this **but**…*"

All the arguments in favour of why you can't do or have what you want starts showing up. You're very adept at listing all the reasons why your desires could never be, and you justify your reasons perfectly with logic, after all, you tell yourself, you're just being "realistic" based on past experiences or what other people have told you is possible.

Or if you're not already introducing reasons why you can't have what you want, you're staying focused on the very reason you launched the rocket of desire in the first place!

The resultant static frequency of resistance then blocks the in-flow of inspiration and ideas. You're not a vibrational match to what you're asking for, so you can't experience it.

The frequent analogy used by Abraham Hicks is you can't have your radio dial tuned to 97.6 FM and hear what is being played on 101 AM.

As you're engaging in thoughts that don't serve you, you may start feeling anxious, disappointed or overwhelmed. The worse you feel, the more your behaviours and actions are affected, and this is when you're likely to fall prey to procrastination, distractions and not taking care of yourself with healthy diet and exercise.

A perfect example of resistance showed up in my experience as inexplicable fatigue!

I was working on my business branding. I'd been in business by this point for 3 years and had never really given much thought to branding. I suppose I didn't really understand it. My business coach Michelle is a branding queen and I was learning so much from her and I was really enjoying it. However, when it came to my own branding and doing the research and creating mood boards, I just hit what felt like a mental brick wall. I was so afraid of getting it wrong!

I scrolled through images and researched other websites and spent hours on Pinterest and nothing seemed to draw me in. I didn't move forward from the branding module for weeks and weeks and I was beyond frustrated. Each time I sat down to work on it, no matter the time of day, I would fall asleep, right there at my desk!

I opened windows, I drank water and coffee and I'd jump up and down to re-energise myself and each time I went back to the branding exercise I found myself overwhelmed with fatigue.

My creativity was non-existent, and I couldn't find inspiration in anything and the more I pushed it, the more mired and irritated I became.

Around this same period, I was considering re-decorating my bedroom. I was starting to get increasingly irritated by the state of it.

5 years ago, when I moved to this property, and became a home improvement ninja, I largely ignored my own bedroom because it didn't feel like a priority at the time. It was the worst room in the house in terms of its aesthetic beauty. The décor was tired and in need of some loving attention and the furniture was ugly to me.

5 years on, I was itching to do something about it, but I just kept putting it off because logically I couldn't justify spending the money on it and besides, I was busy working in and on my business!

One day as I sat at my screen scrolling through images and agonising over my lack of inspiration for my branding, I felt the now-familiar feeling of sleepiness. My eye-lids started to get heavy and my shoulders felt like they had a colossal weight on them! I decided that enough was enough, and although it was 2 0'clock in the afternoon I decided to go to bed.

I set my alarm for an hour, closed the curtains to block out the sun-light and climbed into bed.

Just as I lay down and pulled the duvet up to my chin, the chest of drawers in my bedroom caught my eye. It was an old chest that I'd hand painted some years earlier to give it that "shabby chic" look. There really was nothing chic about it!

I noticed details I hadn't perceived before. The paint work was chipping, and I noticed the dried drips around the base, indicative of my haste to get it done at the time. My eyes darted to the wall behind it and the slap- dash paintwork - work was needed.

Then my eyes were drawn to another part of my bedroom and within moments I was completely alert, eyes wide and mind buzzing with ideas of how I could improve this room. Suddenly, I was full of beans, brimming with excitement by the ideas that were flowing and the order in which I could see everything falling into place.

The difference in my energy was astounding. I wasn't really fatigued at all! I was just in a state of resistance when it came to the work for my business. The impulse and urge to decorate my room was energising and inspiring, but I have to admit, it took me about a week of wrestling with my conscience before I finally gave myself permission to follow my impulse and let go of the "shoulds" and "ought to's". I imagined that I couldn't justify the time off and I was in such a hurry to achieve that elusive state of success that I believed existed somewhere out there.

How wrong I was!!

The moment I released the guilt and got to work in favour of my desires, so much good stuff started happening in my life!

I began by decluttering my wardrobe. I discovered Marie Kondo and her 'Konmari' method of decluttering and organising. It's pretty ruthless, but I loved it! I cleared 70% of my clothing because it was either worn out and tatty, not worn in over a year or it didn't spark joy!

I hired a plasterer to skim the walls and ceiling upstairs and I spent a full week doing what I love! Painting and decorating my home whilst listening to my favourite inspirational speakers and my course training videos.

My heart and mind were open, I felt expansive and creative. I was moving my body and absorbed in the moment. I was in a state of complete joy.

There was no static energy in my frequency!!

Within the space of those 5 days, resources that I'd been wanting for my business for months showed up!! No chasing, no pushing and hustling! They just showed up!

1) Out of the blue my lady who takes care of my tech offered to build me a new website aligned with my new branding, if I would coach her for the next 4 months to help her achieve a big goal she'd set herself. I was thrilled because I'd been wanting a new website for as long as I could remember.

2) A day later a lady contacted me to enquire about my coaching services. I had randomly selected this lady some weeks earlier as part of a prize- draw I had run in my community to win a free 90 minutes coaching session with me. I remember thinking after the session, what a great lady and what she does is exactly what I need for my business (automation and ads!).

    She loved the session and wanted more. She explained that she'd love to invest in my 4 month programme, but funds were tight…I took a chance and suggested the option of an exchange of services and she was thrilled! We both were! It was pure chance that I'd selected her, considering her zone of genius, but joining the dots, it was perfect alignment.

3) I got clarity on my branding – it was like the clouds parted and I knew exactly what my new messaging was and how I wanted my brand to look and feel and then…

4) On day 5 my hairdresser responded to a text message I'd sent her the previous week. I had asked her how much she charged for hair and make-up for a "photo-shoot" since I was up-levelling my brand I wanted some new photos. She asked when my photo- shoot was, and I laughingly replied, "whenever I can get my daughter to take some pictures on her I-phone!" I didn't hear back immediately but then whilst I was up a ladder, paintbrush in hand, following my bliss I got a text from her that said "…I have a great camera…I was going to suggest we do a trade of services as I was thinking about contacting you for some coaching…" and so we did!

As I responded to my guidance, I released the struggle around the branding work. After all, by pushing it I wasn't moving forward and in fact I was blocking progress in other areas of my life and I was just winding myself up into a frazzled mess!

As counterproductive, and counterintuitive, as it seemed in relation to making progress in my business, I started working on my bedroom and it felt amazing! I was buzzing with a renewed energy!

I was literally moving myself to a frequency of creativity, inspiration and productivity. Plus, my blissful state opened up my channels of receptivity to all of those wonderful resources that would escalate my progress.

## DAY 39

Yesterday morning I felt the bubbling up of overwhelm and thought about my workshop copy (big task) and my branding exercises and my NLP work and my client work and I felt the rising up in my chest of anxiety.

I caught it very quickly as I was out walking Joey and knowing how this stuff works, I reached for the next best feeling thought, which was "I always get it all done" ...because...I always do!

As I walked, I affirmed "There's always a right time; I'm loving the clarity that is coming to me around how I want to show up in my brand and I'm enjoying the fact that I'm learning so much about myself and about business from Michelle and it's all happening with perfect timing"

Then in the afternoon I still felt so much resistance to the branding exercise that I fell asleep at my lap-top...Again!!

I took myself off to bed in the middle of the afternoon – my mind whizzing with guilt, so I set my alarm to limit my sleep.

As soon as I lay down on my bed and let go of the tension knowing that I obviously needed to sleep, I started looking around my bedroom – then there was no sleep forthcoming!!

I was no longer tired!! I was excited, and clarity came in around what needed to be done. I lay there thinking "I really should sleep because I was falling asleep at my lap-top just a moment ago…but I really am not tired NOW and I want to get up and start moving stuff around and clearing stuff away in my bedroom and calling the plasterer…" and so I did…and I was not tired one bit.

Recently I've been having so many impulses and desires to clear my bedroom and redecorate – something is so strong about this impulse that I'm going to go with it – although logically I'm telling myself "I don't have time and I don't want to spend the hundreds that I'll need"…and yet that's not me doing what I love to do and following my guidance.

## DAY 44

I implemented the Kon-Mari method to decluttering. It was hugely uplifting. I made some big decisions and have bagged up 70% of my wardrobe in favour of making space and only keeping those things that "spark joy."

I didn't feel so much emotion around my clothes, so I got rid of a lot. I recognised that my attachment came from a place of lack: what if I don't have enough clothes? When I recognised that lack was the source of the feelings of fear, I became even more ruthless.

I even got rid of a lot of the items that Jeremy has bought for me over the years – the first lingerie he even bought me (which now is fraying and tattered! Classy).

A scarf that really isn't my colour or my taste. This felt hard- not because I felt sentimental but because I didn't want to offend him. Again, I had to be conscious and deliberate and if I was going to do this, then I was going to do it properly.

My cupboards are breathy and spacious now and I have a sense that I'll only be wearing nice clothes from now on.

Listening again to Abraham hicks yesterday and the message I heard really resonated with me. Abraham was talking about the creative process. I was thinking about my visibility on-line and creating videos and content. When in the flow of creation – it feels amazing and ideas flow. Those creative ideas were always there but we're just more open to receiving them when we're in that joyful flow state.

I found this to be true – whilst I was enjoying sorting my room, I was bursting with inspired ideas and throughout decluttering I had to keep jotting notes of the ideas I was having!

We can often cut ourselves off from that creative flow state when we spend too long analysing what we've created and wondering (and worrying about) what *others will make of it. Instead we should just keep creating. Stay focused on creating more and more and staying in that high vibe place. I love it!*

So, you see it's critical to do what you love and be in a state of joy and bliss in order to release resistance and get *more* achieved than you ever imagined possible. You're never working alone! Universal forces and an intelligence are always working with you and for you!

The moment you start pushing and forcing results, you're indicating resistance. Pushing and forcing is too much effort and hard work, like pushing a boulder up-hill. There's so much negative energy around it that implies agitation, unease and frustration.

Once I had started the process of exploring how I was responsible for my reality and where my points of resistance were, I started attracting, and enjoying, more clarity!

For example, I began to recognise my huge resistance around *time.* I carried a constant low-level vibration of frustration that there's "never enough hours in the day!"

I'd burst out of the gates every Monday morning full of positive intent about what I was going to achieve that week and by Friday I felt defeated and frustrated for NOT having got *it* all done! It was like Groundhog Day except every week!

I laughed when I realized that of course I never got it all done! I was constantly complaining about never getting it all done, so the Law of Attraction brought me the experience to match my thoughts!

## DAY 46

This has been a very exciting past few days. Pennies are dropping: We are so powerful!!

We have the power to create our reality. It's completely up to us. When I considered Friday's overwhelm and the "reality" that I hadn't got everything done and I was beating myself up, I realised how this particular experience was the physical manifestation of the thoughts and feelings that I've been putting out there consistently!

It's my dominant habit of thought in relation to time. I'm always anxious about time, like there's never enough of the stuff!

Because of that I get stressed out and wind up saying "No" to all the things that fill my cup!

I say "I don't have time" to Joy's invitations to walk Joey-dog together (which means saying no to an hour of stimulating conversation and inspiration that I love), I wind up frustrated at having to break off from work to make a meal and I'm always rushed and impatient!

This means my entire vibration is one of "never enough time to get it all done" so the physical reality is that I don't get it all done! Doh!

Now that I know this, I can switch my focus on to exactly what I want to experience.

Instead of berating myself for 'never enough time', I can choose to celebrate 'more than enough time to achieve all my tasks', knowing that every night I go to bed satisfied and every morning I wake up excited for the day ahead.

I will affirm "I love having the time to focus on my domestic life, my family and my health. I love the gradual unfolding of my business creation and as all the pieces come together with perfect synchronicity, I always feel in control and calm."

*My power in manifesting a PAID IN FULL HSBC card and a PAID IN FULL Halifax card came as a direct result of the power of my focused thought and heightened emotion.*

RESISTANCE:

I've slowed it all down with my Overdraft because I was blocking myself by trying to control the HOW. Instead of focusing on the outcome – which is an account overflowing – I was trying to manipulate the pounds and pence of how I was going to get it to that point. That resulted in me getting impatient and inadvertently focusing on it not happening.

Impatience is a resistant vibration! Impatience is the energy of "I'm not where I want to be!".

I have created a screenshot of my bank balance and whited out the minus sign, so my account looks like it's in credit by £3200.54. That feels so good to imagine my account being in that position. That is where I am going to place my focus every single day.

I've also been stagnant in my ideas and inspiration around my branding because I've been stuck in the HOW. How do I want it to look? How do I afford the photo-shoot and photography? How do I decide on the final look? How? How? How?

Focusing on the 'how' keeps me in the energy of more questions, and less clarity! As my Coach Hasnaa says, don't focus on the how, focus on the 'what', that is the end result.

## DAY 50

This past week has been "tight" as I've had nothing coming in and was a little too hasty on the slashing of the O/D facility. Whilst I am happy that I've got it down from £3500 to £1500 I feel a little constricted.

However, there have been 2 major celebrations! Firstly, that there were moments this week when I thought of buying something and facing the consequences afterwards, by taking credit from somewhere. All to please others mind you!

None of the purchases were really about me and since I stopped myself, I'm celebrating that I'm breaking that unconscious habitual pattern. I'm affirming instead that "I'm savvy and I'm choosing to save my money".

Second was a realisation that as I'm chronicling this journey, I'm really learning how to smooth the bumps in the road to alignment. Alignment being that joyful state of ZERO resistance.

Reducing my overdraft facility and being left uncomfortably tight, is a lesson in the perils of attempting to push the result. I was trying to control how it's going to happen rather than trusting the Universe. By slashing my overdraft and trying to control this rather than feeling abundant and ensuring that I'm easily able to pay all of my bills – I put myself in to a restricted state.

I spent a lot of the past 48 hours getting back into alignment through visualising the outcome and seeing the overflowing balance in my bank account and picturing stamping my Barclaycard statement and my Bank of Scotland statement with the big red "PAID IN FULL" stamp!

I then was imagining all the delicious ways that I could repay mum and Paul their £10k. I then saw this book – published and wrapped for Jeremy.

As I did this practice, I felt such immense joy and I love knowing that I am thinking my way into a new state of being.

I love knowing that through this continuous daily practice I am creating new neural connections and my body is "memorising" an abundant state.

As I'm experiencing being free from debt on a daily basis, I'm becoming someone who is always in a state of alignment and easily recognises when she's' "off" and therefore can shift right back into alignment.

I love doing this. It's coming so easily to me and feels so great.

## DAY 51

I'm returning to my daily gratitude practice after the discipline waivered a little and having been away for a short break – I managed to maintain my visualisation practice and really enjoyed getting viscerally connected to the joy of the moment whilst in my visualisation.

It's easy to wobble and waiver – this is perfectly natural. I am changing lifelong habits and losing an old identity in order to develop a new and more empowering personality. I am developing an entirely new state of being around the subject of money.

I am free from debt – I am Paid in Full

I am smart and savvy – I am an excellent money manager I enjoy budgeting and being organised around money

I speak openly and without shame on the topic of money

I can show up with integrity and in my highest and best self

I'm beginning to feel inspired and called to make more upgrades to my home décor I want my environment to reflect some of the changes as I'm growing and evolving as a person.

This house is MY beautiful home and a metaphor for any challenge I face in the future. This home really was the making of me as I tapped into my brilliant potential and became unstoppable in pursuit of the worthy cause – to not only make this house a home, but also to make this place something I can feel truly proud and accomplished in. To make my children comfortable and proud. To want to be here and feel good about being here.

This helped me push through the tough times in my business. There have been times in my business when things seemed hopeless and I cried. These were painful moments – part of me knew that my meltdowns were clearing a way to think more resourcefully and creatively but at the same time I cried from feelings of acute rejection and dejection.

How was I ever going to make this work? I'd feel swamped, overwhelmed and powerless. But then I'd remember how I tackled the mammoth task of making this house a home, how I stepped up to the plate time and time again, despite so many difficulties at the time.

Throughout this process I have come to realise how much I have been sabotaging my progress – beating myself up; resisting making a daily to do list and getting deeply emotional and attached to every outcome.

As I'm releasing the negative emotion and letting go of the resistance, I'm able to implement the strategy and take massive <u>aligned</u> action on behalf of myself, my business and my clients.

## DAY 56

I have created a sense of relaxation around "time" which is huge! The resistance is easing after just 2 weeks of affirming that I have more than enough time!! I feel so productive. Repetition! Repetition! Repetition! What a game-changer!

I'm appreciative of the journey and I'm way more sensitive to my feelings.

Normally I would push aside such 'frivolous activities', such as decorating my house, in favour of working on my business but yesterday I found myself getting all balled up inside over a corner of my living room – yep! A corner!

I was really getting irritated by how ugly it was and no matter what pictures and vases I arranged in it, I still found it ugly!

As I was stood facing this corner, my head tilted with fists on hips and feeling very distracted, Jeremy asked me to drive him to work. Perfect timing! In leaving the house and giving space to my thoughts, I realised that what my living room corner needed was a new colour! I decided there and then that I needed to paint the wall.

That was it!! Instant joy and bliss at the prospect of more painting whilst giving me the perfect opportunity to plug it to my Abraham Hicks audios! This instantaneous good feeling was too good to ignore. So, I took the necessary detour, bought the paint and started my mini project.

After decorating my bedroom, I feel like I've got the decorating bug again!! Ha!

More Exciting news!!

A week ago I thought to myself "I could do with £1000 – I could do with that amount to cover my mortgages next week" – I felt pretty confident that I could do that although I had started getting a little angsty about the prospect of having to use my credit cards...eeek!! I managed to rationalise that I still have 5 days to make this money, before all my main outgoings were due.

On day 3 of the 5, I messaged a prospect about an offer of coaching for £997. No response. On the evening of the 4th working day (Thursday) I journaled on my power to create and I set a broad and non-specific intention for the next day, Friday, to be an awesome day. I was going to have a wonderful day and I got excited.

That Friday, I received £997 and my bank account hasn't looked this abundant and healthy in such a long time! And all my bills are covered and then some.

I am loving playing these games and I'm excited by my ability to create whatever I want.

I was nervous about taking time away from my business to paint my home because I was impatient and rushing to achieve my goals. Impatience carries a vibration of "I'm not there yet" and is coming from a negative place and keeps you stuck right where you are. Whenever you begin to feel impatient, appreciate and bless where you are now with excitement for your continued progress.

**Call to Action:**

**When you experience resistance in your vibration, the fastest ways to release are to:**

**Change the subject**

**Quite literally take yourself away from the subject that is causing the resistance. You may choose to meditate to quiet the thoughts or go**

for a walk or run with music or with a friend who you can talk about anything with (of course anything that isn't the topic causing resistance!)

You can go and take a nap if the thoughts are so distracting and you have a lot of momentum behind them. Taking a nap resets your vibration so long as when you wake up you don't immediately focus back on the problem.

Align with the vibrational frequency of what you want to achieve, by doing something easier that has a matching frequency (like I wanted to get creative with my branding but I was stuck, so I got creative with decorating my bedroom and that put me in an aligned state to receive the ideas for my brand - and of course I received a whole lot more too!)

e.g. 1) Perhaps you're feeling out of control and you're stuck on that frequency in relation to your money and debt management. You want to feel in control but right now, where money is concerned, it's too big a leap vibrationally.

Seek easier baby-step ways to perpetuate feelings of being in control. For example, where else around your home or office could you act to assert more control? Perhaps there's an "out of control" drawer full of paper work or a hazardous shoe cupboard that needs sorting. Take the necessary action and organise it to raise your "in control" frequency. Notice your great time- keeping and celebrate your healthy food choices in which you exercised control. With practice and a little bit of time, "being in control" will become your dominant vibration.

e.g. 2) Perhaps you're beating yourself up for having an unproductive week, like I was, and that is keeping you in a vibration of *stuck*. Then seek out ways that you can match your vibration to that of increased productivity.

Affirm productivity and find some smaller tasks that you can act on with ease that helps you feel productive.

# Slaying the Saboteurs

I used the analogy of starting this journey by programming the GPS in your car to your destination and the importance of knowing your starting point.

You're going somewhere new, which means you're alert and constantly tracking your guidance system with your current location to ensure you're heading in the right direction.

It's important to remain vigilant, unlike that daily drive to work or taking the kids to school! You know what it's like, sometimes you arrive to your familiar destination and realise that you have no recollection of the journey! Your mind and body are habituated to the route and therefore your mind is free to wander.

However, now you're embarking on a brand-new journey into unfamiliar territory and this requires your focused attention and awareness of all the forks and bumps in the road.

These forks and bumps in the road are what could potentially derail you. These are what I call the saboteurs.

Saboteurs can be the stories that we tell ourselves every day or they can be our subconscious beliefs – either way they're like heat seeking missiles in that they fall under the radar and yet cause so much damage!

This is where a daily journal becomes your closest ally and your map-reading travel buddy!

Your journal is where you document your progress, your results, your thoughts and your feelings every day in relation to your journey to destination 'Paid in Full'.

Journaling with intention every day will support this work very powerfully. Since your intention is to invite more prosperity into your life and become Paid in Full, journaling will keep you focused on the goal.

Furthermore, your daily journal will become an accurate reflection of your dominant thoughts, feelings, activities and outcomes.

Everything you need to raise self-awareness and pull back the curtain on your saboteurs and limiting stories. Understand too that The Law of Attraction is at work and what you're attracting, whether wanted or not, is a reflection of your dominant thoughts and beliefs.

As you journal ask yourself:

**What current stories do I tell myself (and others) about myself, that do not serve me?** You'll know they don't serve you because they're the stories that NEVER feel good!

For example, I used to constantly refer to myself as undisciplined. I used to say: "*I can't plan or stick to a schedule!*"; "*I never stick at things*" and "*I leave everything to the last minute…*"

Telling myself, and believing, that I was undisciplined was a real problem for me because running my own business meant that I had to self-manage.

I always felt so ridiculously busy and chaotic and every week I'd get to Friday and I'd beat myself up for not getting everything done that I wanted. I'm talking every *single* Friday!

169

My coaches would constantly tell me to schedule in my self-care and regular tasks like grocery shopping and I would do it. I scheduled it in my calendar…that didn't mean they got done!!

I'd wind up busy at my desk, engrossed in busy-ness and the fridge and kitchen cupboards went bare.

This went on for a couple of years, since I started my business. I'd have little self-discipline 'blips' where I'd get so frustrated that I'd force myself to stick to the schedule and for a week or two. During those times I felt great! I was completing all my tasks, I was on top of my domestic chores, I was doing my exercise and taking breaks. Clearly the way forward! *"Yay! I've nailed it!"* I'd say!

But then within a couple of weeks I'd have a bad day when I'd fall off the wagon. It could be as simple as a client call running over time (that I allowed to happen instead of having the firm boundary and respecting my schedule). As the over-run cut into the time allotted for my next task, for example, the run I'd scheduled between calls, I would drop the run, so I wouldn't be late for the next call. I knew I could go for a shorter run of course, that would be the sensible and logical thing to do.

But by then, the little chatter in my head would start to kick in "Y*ou're rubbish you are! You're so undisciplined! There's no way you can stick to this schedule, you've messed it up already…"* And then I'd backslide right back into the chaos.

I believed my own story, as much as it made me feel bad, I thought it was who I was at my core. To try to force myself to change kicked up a storm as my subconscious mind felt threatened and I'd sabotage my best efforts.

Also, because I constantly beat myself up for being undisciplined, and every Friday I'd feel unhappy with where I was, and how "little" I'd accomplished (by my standards that is!) Law of Attraction brought me more of the same. So, my reality never changed!

## Change the Story.

I remember thinking *can it really be as simple as changing the stories you're telling yourself?* And the answer is simply YES! The everyday things you think and say about yourself and to yourself are like embedded commands to your brain.

171

Your brain is simply acting on instruction. "I am_____" are two of the most powerful words in the English language because whatever adjective follows becomes your point of focus and therefore your point of attraction.

You will attract more thoughts, situations and circumstances that match your point of focus. Then you can say "See? I told you I am_____" because the evidence is there.

I love the analogy of our brains being like the search engine, Google. Whatever we type into the search bar, Google will bring back all the references that match our search words.

I used to say, "I am undisciplined". Whenever I thought that thought, it was like I was typing "I am undisciplined" into Google because my Google brain would immediately bring up as many references and evidence to validate that statement.

Like a flash, I'd recall, with a lurching sensation in my stomach how many failed attempts I'd made at sticking to a schedule. I would remember the time I gave up alcohol for a month and on day 28 I caved in and had a glass of wine, enjoying it but all the time feeling like a loser. I would consider my credit card balances and feel terrible, confirmation indeed that I was undisciplined and out of control.

Nothing positive would come from my Google brain and so my limiting belief would be reinforced as my truth. I would feel disempowered around schedules and plans and shut down my natural states of resourcefulness and possibility.

There's no truth in my statement really. It's simply a matter of focus and my past chronic patterns of thought.

I can choose to tell myself "I am disciplined". I can focus on that statement and deliberately affirm it until I start attracting thoughts that match.

Of which, there are as many positive anecdotes of discipline as there are negative ones of being undisciplined!

For example: I trained myself to run the London Marathon which meant running every morning at 5am; I studied my A'level Biology whilst working full time and having 7 year old twins which required an almost military amount of discipline; I have certificates on my wall of qualifications that I have passed which all required discipline and scheduling.

It's simply a matter of choosing the more empowering stories to create more empowering beliefs that ultimately direct you to create your best life.

Realising that you have a choice moment to moment on where you place your focus is ultimately where your power lies.

The more you practice observing and listening and deliberating choosing to focus your attention on what you want, the stronger and increasingly self - aware you become. It's rather like exercising a muscle. Over time, what you want to experience, whether it's more discipline, or just more happiness and satisfaction becomes your default dominant vibration. You also notice and catch yourself earlier in the process if you're unconsciously thinking negative thoughts because you're more tuned in to your vibration and your emotional guidance system.

**Call to Action:**

**What stories do you tell about yourself that do not serve you?**

**What beliefs do you have that are disempowering?**

## What new stories do you need to start telling yourself to override these beliefs?

## DAY 61

I sometimes get nervous before a live-stream because I have thoughts that sound like "I get too deep" and I start "talking shit".

I regularly feel overwhelmed and the churning starts in the pit of my stomach because I am thinking "I am so busy – I have so much to do".

I frequently berate myself for not being as productive, and I feel impatient with myself and the thoughts I'm thinking are "I am not where I want to be"

I chose now to write out in vivid detail EXACTLY how I want to feel and think in these areas of my life and continue to place my focus there and affirm it until I start to notice the evidence in favour of the new truth – the reality that I am creating:

I am a confident and brilliant speaker – I am engaging and inspiring and I attract people who love and value what I say and who resonate with my words powerfully

I always take focused action and achieve incredible momentum and complete all my tasks on time – I never allow social media to distract me

I always have enough time in my day to get it done

I stick to the important tasks and disciplines that have the biggest impact on my results in every area of my life

I am always celebrating!! Celebrating all of my wins because that sets me up for more and more. I acknowledge my growth and my progress.

I easily assert what I want when it comes to making requests for help and support from my children. I love the ease and flow of the running of the household and everyone pulls together.

I always put content out into the world from an inspired place – I know that the power comes from the inspired energy.

I love how money flows to me and I am growing more and more wealthy every single day.

# Your Results Never Lie

By the very nature of our subconscious beliefs, they're submerged, hidden and difficult to interpret by conscious thought alone.

However, since everything originates from thought, you can shine a spotlight on your subconscious patterns of thought by observing and interpreting your results. What are you creating? What results are you 'attracting' into your life on a consistent basis, whether wanted or not wanted? And more importantly, how can you change with more ease?

Remember, the law of attraction is a governing law of the universe. Just like gravity, it is never not at play. People say "Meh, the law of attraction doesn't work for me" when they don't get what they want, but the law of attraction is never not working.

The Law of Attraction is constantly responding to the frequency of your

vibration which is being determined
by your thoughts and your feelings.

You are the creator of your reality moment to
moment and what you attract as experiences
are always a match to your dominant
vibrational frequency. What you think about,
you bring about.

I told you that I had one of my biggest
breakthroughs during one of my challenging
times, so let me share it with you. It's mind-
blowing in its simplicity and yet powerful as
an example to help you shift your
subconscious blocks and attract more of what
you want.

At the outset of my journey to becoming
Paid in Full, I committed to a daily ritual
of gratitude journaling, visualising and
focusing on money and abundance.

Within 5 days of starting, I fell off the wagon for
a few days. I beat myself up, I exerted force and
got back on the horse. This became a regular
occurrence. Sometimes I didn't do any daily
practice for a week and then I'd beat myself up,
exert force and get back on the horse again!

Hardly a high vibe I know, but I was
frustrated! I felt as though all those things
that I enjoyed, and I knew were good for me,

I couldn't keep up with! It made no sense. But I continued to push through with effort because I was chronicling the journey – thank goodness I was too, otherwise I may well have quit!

Anyway, I had enjoyed 4 consecutive months of great income in my business up to this point. My journaling, visualisation and gratitude practice was reaping rewards and I was happy. Yet month 5, it all stopped! I was aware that I had fallen off my daily practice wagon of late, but I still felt good!

I couldn't believe that it would have such an immediate impact on my business results! I was still 'showing up' and being active. It was a mystery to me and I didn't know what to do except to continue my action taking with increased faith.

A few weeks earlier, following a fun self-awareness exercise that I did with my coach I recognised that I wanted to bring back running into my daily routine. I was a runner for 10 years, enjoying taking part in half marathons every year. My business had taken over my life and I lost sight of the importance of looking after myself – not surprising then that as I was burning out, I was taking my business down with me!

I made an important decision to re-introduce a daily run into my schedule and I was excited, I even bought new trainers in readiness!

7 days into my new running routine and I felt great…14 days in I was feeling on top of the world – strong, disciplined, in control…then day 20… BAM! I took a clumsy step and twisted my right ankle! It felt pretty bad in the moment, but I still managed to continue running a little way further before deciding that it was probably wise to turn back and head home.

During the rest of that day my ankle swelled up and I experienced excruciating pain. I couldn't weight bear at all and I couldn't drive, so I called a taxi and went to the emergency ward at the local hospital to get it checked out. After some checks and an X-Ray, it turned out I had torn my ankle ligament and needed to rest. No strenuous activity for at least a couple of weeks was the recommendation.

I was beyond frustrated. I was so enjoying the benefits to my mind, body and soul of being out every day, getting my heart pumping and my muscles moving…it was as though I'd been reunited with running and I was loving it!

I spent a week feeling sorry for myself and I slowed down in my business productivity too as I hobbled about wondering "how have I attracted this torn ligament?" I was confused because I thought that I must have been thinking about injuries or ill-health to attract this, but I knew that I hadn't had any thoughts of that sort at all!

Before long I began to sit up and ask the question "how have I attracted this?" with more determination and the intention of receiving an answer.

The answer came to me whilst I was messaging my coach to request a quick chat. I wanted a loving kick up the butt because whilst my ankle was preventing me from running, it was no excuse for my inactivity in my business! I was writing about my thoughts and feelings around my ankle injury when I recognised that what I was describing were familiar patterns of thought and feeling that I've had about other areas of my life.

I described feeling frustrated, held back and slow. I wrote that I hated not being able to keep up with everyone and I worried about falling behind because of my limping; I complained that my injury had stopped me from sticking to my routine of running and discipline and I explained my disappointment and annoyance at stopping after such a buoyant and positive beginning!

I know! What a bundle of joy I was! Luckily for my coach I didn't press send, because like a lightening bolt I received such breakthrough clarity.

I *had* attracted my torn ligament because I had a chronic pattern of thought that I recognised immediately as "I never stick at anything." I had that in my vibration for years.

The torn ligament was an exact match to my dominant vibrational pattern of frustration from "never sticking at things".

I only had to look at the results I had created in other areas of my life to realise this to be true for me. The many half read books on my shelves, the courses and personal development programmes I've started and ditched mid-way, the various healthy eating regimes I've embarked on fanatically only to let fall by the way side and fizzle out! Not to mention the amount of times I've attempted to commit to a schedule to manage my workload only to not stick to the plan and then lament that I'm undisciplined!

# How you do anything is how you do everything

As the realisation took hold, I began to consider the wider implications of this belief that *I never stick at anything.* I was subconsciously creating inconsistency in my business results too!

I realised that my pattern in my business was that I would do the necessary activity that I knew brought in the money for several months with enthusiasm and energy. I'd start seeing results and celebrating and relaxing into it. Then, seemingly inexplicably after 4 or 5 months, the clients and cash would stop flowing and I couldn't understand why.

I was *still* taking the necessary action. On a conscious level at least, I believed I was still showing up every day and doing what I needed to do. And yet the steady flow stopped.

On a subconscious level I sabotaged my results to match my story of "I never stick at anything". I created feast and famine in my business!

I cannot count the amount of times I've had to "give myself a stern talking to and get back on the horse" and I've always done it but only after I'd driven myself into a deep enough ditch to give myself the necessary motivation!

Your results are always a vibrational match to your dominant frequency. It's law and it cannot be any other way.

DAY 130:

PROSPERITY IS A TAP THAT I CAN TURN ON AND OFF!!

Welcome to day 130 and a massive BREAKTHROUGH realisation – my chronic way of thinking is that I never stick at anything!!

I have been looking at my results and wondering what has switched off the tap of income flowing compared to the previous 4 consistent months.

I've been agonising over "what is my limiting belief here?" Trying to figure out what is my upper limiting problem that stops me stepping up into my zone of genius AKA creating consistent results and being amazing and achieving my goals!

My realisation came to me from a curve ball.

I started running again at the start of month 5. Less than 3 weeks in I tore my ankle ligament and that put paid to my running for the next 2 weeks. I've barely been off my backside at all now for just over 2 weeks!

As I focused on understanding how I attracted this and what this torn ligament experience was revealing to me about my point of attraction, I realised with total clarity that my chronic way of thinking and self-admonishment and self-judgement and criticism is all because "I never stick at anything"…and so I attracted an exact match to stop me from sticking to my running.

Equally – when I look at my morning routine of gratitude journaling, of visualising and chronicling the journey…it stopped being consistent after about 60 days – it became hit and miss and then to practically a halt.

The mindset at the time was "hey this is working and so I can stop" but WHY STOP THE ONE THING THAT IS WORKING!!??? It just doesn't make sense…but it's a saboteur, a subconscious belief / pattern that I never stick at anything.

This is a big win as AWARENESS is the first step to change. My work now is:

To be kind to myself i.e. no frustration and self-judgement – after all I don't know what I don't know.

To celebrate the clarity and awareness because this is BIG

To respect my tracker calendar (it's really scribbled on and random notes all over!!)

To re-print fresh new credit card statements and write a new statement of affirmation on them

To write every day my gratitude journal

To visualise my credit cards being paid in full

To read this book!! There is so much GOLD here! Ha ha!

I also want to find evidence every day of disciplines and ways of being that prove to me that I can and DO stick at things!

Right now, that feels hard however if I dig a bit:

- My Business! I stick at my business and my daily posting and commitment to showing up everyday

- I stick at my commitment to having a sit-down meal as a family and creating that positive habit.

- I stick at maintaining my positive mindset and have transformed the way I think

- I stuck at my A'Level Biology – no matter how hard it was – I was disciplined, and I passed!

- I stuck at completing the renovations for my house, not only making it habitable but also beautiful!

My chronic way of thinking seems to be related to **daily** disciplines. Last week I watched a live stream that a fellow coach did on Facebook. She was sharing an inspirational story about a guy she'd met at an event. He was a speaker and he told his story of how he went from being an alcoholic to completing the Iron Man!

The coach was so impressed by his incredible story of endurance and perseverance in the face of many adversities and challenges. During the question section this coach raised her hand and asked him how he managed to keep going and not give up during those moments when it felt tough. He just replied by saying he took every day as it came, one day at a time with the mantra "If I can just do it today"

If I didn't think about the bigger and more onerous task of doing this every day for ever...that might be what feels crushing...If

I just told myself that I am going to do this today. Get up at 5am and do my daily practices and my run today. Until it becomes weird **not** to AND until I reach a point when NOT doing it becomes painful.

Maybe I need another Calendar to mark off a big red cross every day that I complete the activities. That's what I'm going to do now. Order another calendar.

New affirmation:

I love sticking to my daily success activities that feel good are fun and take me exactly where I want to go!! Yippppeeeee!! I'm riding that bus from now on!!!

This awareness meant that anytime I attempted to block myself from doing my daily disciplines or sticking to things, I was able to make a conscious choice about it. I could just say to myself "Uh Oh! Hello saboteur! Not today thank you!"

I also affirmed my new chosen story everyday *"I AM disciplined! I love how easy it feels to stick to those daily activities that feel so good to me! I always finish what I start!"*

190

Call to Action:

What specifically are the unsatisfactory results in your experience? (e.g. You've attracted a huge and unexpected bill that has to be paid)

Analyse those results. What are they reflecting to you? (e.g. Perhaps the bill is reflecting back lack, fear of spending money, being unprepared)

What is the emotional essence of the experience? (e.g. Perhaps the bill is making you feel defeated)

What are those emotions revealing to you about your point of focus? (As you feel defeated you might realise that your point of focus is on "I'll never get on top of my finances; life's full of nasty surprises; I'll never have enough money")

Take a moment to zoom out of the experience to give you a broader perspective. (in the case of the unexpected bill and how it makes you feel defeated, you might begin to notice other areas of your life where you might feel defeated regularly, like your pile of paperwork or your taxes that you're never able to get on-top of or perhaps you constantly worry about never having enough money!)

Once you've isolated the chronic thought pattern you can follow my steps to change it:

**Step 1)** Be kind and compassionate with yourself rather than self- admonishing and critical

**Step 2)** Celebrate the clarity and the awareness! Not only are you focusing on clarity and awareness but the celebration that feels so wonderful attracts in more of the same!

**Step 3)** Take action! What needs to happen immediately for you to address the situation?

**Step 4)** Re-write your story! Write out a new and affirming statement that acts as the antidote to the original limiting story and place your focus on it

**Step 5)** Find new evidence! As you focus on the new and more empowering story, write a list of at least 5 situations that act as evidence and references in favour of the new story.

*DAY 131*

So much truth has emerged through this incredible process! Our prosperity is a tap that we can turn on and turn off – we are so powerful. Looking back in 2016 when I "turned my tap off" I know now that I stopped doing my gratitude journaling and I started taking my income for granted.

After a few months of struggle, I turned the tap back on again in February 2017 and then my subconscious pattern of "I never stick at things" threw me under the bus again months later. Only that time, I didn't know what I know now, and I kept spiralling downhill.

## DAY 132

Don't be an observer – be a visionary. When we are observers – we're looking at 'what is' – but 'what is' is already a manifestation.

By holding your attention to it – you trigger your default reaction that perpetuates the same emotional response which dictates your actions and behaviours (and the frequency at which you're vibrating) hence getting the same results

193

over and over and attracting more "evidence" to 'prove' your belief to you.

I am a visionary – and I am envisioning time, time and more time and getting everything I want done!

I am a visionary and I am envisioning myself serving more and more clients and experiencing the joy of a full booked academy programme

I am a visionary and I am envisioning money flowing in to me and all my bills paid with thanks

I am a visionary and I am envisioning the growing wealth and the bulging bank account

I am a visionary and I am envisioning the prosperity that I am experiencing in health, wealth, love and light. I am a visionary and I am envisioning the lightness of my being

I am a visionary and I am envisioning the clarity and the confidence

I am a visionary and I am envisioning the joy, the joy, the joy! Oh, the Joy of it all!

## DAY 137

As I shared my celebrations with Hasnaa, my excitement at my recent breakthroughs and the realisation at how powerful I am, of how powerful we ALL are, Hasnaa and I talked about what's next for me.

The focus became this book.

Hasnaa helped me to connect to my heart and the answers that my heart held in relation to the question of "so what now?". My heart screamed out – share this! Share this!! There are millions of people in the world whose lives could be turned around if they only realised how powerful they are.

And perhaps I can tell it in my way, with my voice, wrapped in my story and that it would resonate with some, where previous stories haven't.

What am I an expert in? I'm an expert in the accumulation of debt. I've spent the past 23 years in the industry of managing and accumulating credit card debt. 23 years in a toxic relationship with debt and finally broken free from the toxicity of it all.

I finally understand "The Secret".

I know that words don't teach, and that people need to experience this in order to really know it. But there has to be a level of awareness of what to look for, which is what I can share.

People need to know how to interpret their experiences in order to shine a light on what is really going on and to get closer to the truth of who they really are and what they're capable of.

So, my heart was bursting with the message "Get this out there!" I felt scared and Hasnaa assured me that it was because it's the right thing to do. I want to feel the exhilaration and excitement of being outside of my comfort zone – knowing that I'm always supported – that it can never go wrong – it really can never go wrong.

# The God in Me is Me

At around the 6-month mark of my journey, I experienced another significant turning point that further deepened my appreciation of this whole experience.

When I started this journey, it was entirely about repaying my debts. I knew that I had to breakthrough limiting beliefs and subconscious patterns that were perpetuating my situation.

I knew that. I imagined it would be hard and part of me was afraid that I would achieve my goal, but still have that old germ of a debt seed inside of me. That perhaps I'd fall back into my old patterns helplessly…and we'd meet again in year or two and I'd be deeper in debt than ever!!

I was unconsciously postponing joy because I believed that I needed to be debt free in order to fully enjoy my life.

I was prepared to do the work, whatever it took to free myself.

What I wasn't expecting was the depth of immersion and understanding of The Law of Attraction. Everything made perfect sense to me and I really was getting a handle on how powerful we are as humans, to create our own reality.

The holes in my knowledge in this respect were getting filled and I was beyond excited that I was developing my sensitivities and ability to interpret my feelings and my results.

Whenever I experienced a negative feeling or an unsatisfactory result, I was all over it! I was having so much fun!

I was helping my clients too! At the end of a fun and insightful session during which I helped my client discover her limiting pattern of thought she said to me *"Sanae, I love how your brain works!"*

I realised that I had changed how I think. I had created shifts in how my brain processes information and it felt so empowering.

Then I awakened even more. A simple realisation that felt like the icing on the cake of this whole enlightening process occurred around 6 months in. We were on the motorway, Jeremy in the driving seat, heading for a week away in a quaint English cottage in The Cotswolds. Bliss! I was excited to be spending a week with everyone together as we'd arranged this break with mum and her husband, Paul.

As we were bombing down the motorway Jeremy accidently missed our motorway exit. We both did that "Oh! How did that happen?" thing as we looked from the sat-nav to the road and back to the sat-nav.

We drove for a bit in silence, Jeremy fully focused on where next to exit and I sensed his agitation. I listened in and observed my own thoughts and feelings, I was happily unattached to the situation.

An alternative exit soon showed up and Jeremy took it.

Within moments we were winding through the most stunning countryside I'd ever seen! There were hardly any other cars on the road as we meandered through quaint cottage lined villages separated by beautiful rolling fields of varying hues of yellows and greens. Nothing fuels my soul like the English countryside and I felt my spirit up-lift. I was already pretty high, but this was internal joy on a whole other level! I felt replete with well-being. My head was like it was on a swivel as I feasted on the views on every side of the car! It was ecstasy!

Suddenly the words "*I did this*" popped into my head. "*I did this!*" I felt my heart expanding as I realised that I was a cooperative component in creating this joyful experience. I had "realised" this moment, manifested it and more importantly perceived it fully because I was in that high vibration place of receiving.

The week-long break that followed was perfect in every way. The cottage was picture perfect, the sun shone every single day, I ran every morning with my son and Jeremy and we all chatted and laughed and had a wonderful time. The words *"I did this!"* kept popping in to my head and I'd find myself smiling to myself and feeling a warmth that felt like love.

What became clear to me as a result of this experience, was that I was receiving joy more fully.

Yes, I was making progress! Yes, I was reducing my debt balance! Yes, I was signing clients and making more money than I ever had before! Yes, I knew what to do in the face of resistance and self-sabotage!

But the real breakthrough? My capacity for receiving and perceiving joy was greater than I'd ever allowed it to be. I was expanded. In that expanded space, was total self-acceptance.

I had moved my needle from shame and self-loathing to worthiness and love; from not enough to more than enough and from chaos and burn- out to calm and balance.

We returned home from the holiday, and I got back to business. Within a matter of weeks, I was celebrating smashing my monthly target (I made £29,000 that month to be exact)! I cleared my overdraft, my 2nd largest credit card and set up a standing order to pay mum back. I also invested in my joy too, such as a 4 day mini-break to Portugal and a trip to visit with Infinite Intelligence aka Abraham Hicks.

My journaling took on a different tone at this point. I was doing a lot less scrutinising and analysing as I caught up with myself and allowed myself to settle into this new expanded sense of self. My daily journaling became more like positive streams of consciousness, as I allowed my joy and excitement to guide my fingers on the keyboard. The words were repetitive, high energy and high vibration and I just allowed whatever was flowing through me to be written on the page.

## DAY 167

I'm not yet fully debt free, but I have reached the state of being Paid in Full, in every other way! My cup is full.

It's so freaking exciting. I get it now! There is no hurry, everything has a divine timing and I am still on my journey. My new truth and reality are that I am wealthy, worthy and wise. I feel my whole body light up as I know that my new truth and my new reality is that I am worthy, wealthy and wise.

This is it. I am a powerful creator of my reality and I am excited to play games with the Universe. I get to choose from the catalogue of the Universe anything and everything I desire, safe and secure in the knowledge that I can create it.

I am so happy and grateful for every experience I have lived up to now, that has made me wise to my worthiness. I am grateful to every one of my amazing clients who I love so much.

Spirited women determined to achieve incredible results. I am here to guide and support them and I am excited for them. I love and respect them as they love and respect me.

I love being creative and expressive and expansive.

I know that I am growing and becoming the person that I was always born to be. I am happy and whole exactly as I am. My life is a success and I am successful now. I am creating my reality and playing the game of life.

I love knowing that every step of my journey enables me to become stronger in my capacity to help others. I love supporting others as I myself, am supported. I am loved. I am worthy. I am a worthy and wealthy woman.

I am expanding every single day – every single day I am expanding my perceptions of what is possible for me.

I am a powerful creator. I get it! I get it!! I get it!!! I am a powerful creator and I attract in everything that is a match to my dominant vibration – I am vibrating at the frequency of wealth, joy and abundance.

I am having fun. I expect everything that I want to come to me – maybe not today and maybe not tomorrow but it's coming. All of the cooperative components are gathering and joining forces and I am open and noticing all the possibilities and the infinite potential of the amazing infinite intelligence in which we are all existing…everything I want exists in potential and as I focus, I gather the energy to create anything and everything I want.

I am almighty powerful – the god in me is my own intelligent power.

The god in me is ME!!!

The god in me is ME!!!

I have the ability and wherewithal to solve all of my problems - I just have to listen, observe and take note of how I feel and what my intuition is telling me and then I am guided.

I am guided. The god in me is me. I am floating in a universe of infinite possibilities and potential and as I focus my attention, I become a deliberate creator. I will experience my desires because I choose to and when I focus deliberately, I create it. I draw all the cooperative components and their matching frequencies that cause it to become visible to me. I am a powerful creator and what I believe is what I perceive. I choose to believe in my wealth and prosperity. It's already done...and as soon as my focused and dominant vibration becomes a match, I will experience it with my senses.

I love my life. I love this life.

At this point I started to feel like I wanted to share what I had learned so far and whilst there is still some remaining debt, that's OK. It's very OK.

I used to think there would be no value in publishing a book to help others become free of debt if I hadn't yet attained that position. I believed that I'd be lacking integrity in fact.

I know now that that's not true. I have gained so much more in this process than simply becoming debt free and I hope if you followed this and took the actions, you will experience this value too.

The point is that you can change your mindset so that you're no longer unconsciously perpetuating debt.

You can eliminate the burden of shame and neutralise the intense negative emotions that you have around money and debt. You can recognise and release your limiting patterns of thought that diminish your potential.

You can forgive yourself and move into a state of self-compassion and self-acceptance. You can expand your capacity to experience joy in your day to day life and spend time appreciating the creative role you play in all of your happy moments.

You can trust your instincts, your impulses and your emotional guidance system. You can develop an empowered state of mind that fuels your confidence to take positive action and respond to what feels right and good.

And you can enjoy the journey of reducing your debt balance, without postponing joy.

That in fact, when you are in joy, doing what you love and taking inspired action that feels good, you have already achieved your true desired state.

Love

Sanae x

# Notes & Reflections

# Notes & Reflections

# Notes & Reflections

# Notes & Reflections

Printed in Great Britain
by Amazon